# THREE E[NGLISH PLAYS]

❀

Larins Sahib

Mira

9 Jakhoo Hill

*More praise for the book*

'Remarkable in the way [*Mira*] combined Indian legend with the sophistication of Western total theatre.... [It] has something of the quality of dream ritual.'                                    — Clive Barnes, *The New York Times*

'But, by all that is noble and true, this is really no "experiment", but an artistic achievement of immense merit and supreme significance to the re-blossoming of the theatre in India.... A rare, beautiful experience, watching and listening to *Mira*; one came out of the theatre cleaner, more joyous, and several centimetres taller.'                     — *Times of India*

'The story [of *9 Jakhoo Hill*] weaves around a family who stays at the Shimla address, circa 1962, during the summer of discontent for a once-wealthy clan, brooding over better days.... It's more of an insight than a message ... on the hold that mothers have over their sons, a family coming down in the world ... remnants of the Raj, disillusionment with politics. Sixties? The script is here and now.'                     — *India Today*

# THREE ENGLISH PLAYS

Larins Sahib

Mira

9 Jakhoo Hill

## GURCHARAN DAS

OXFORD
UNIVERSITY PRESS

# OXFORD
UNIVERSITY PRESS

YMCA Library Building, Jai Singh Road, New Delhi 110 001

Oxford University Press is a department of the University of Oxford. It furthers th
University's objective of excellence in research, scholarship, and education
by publishing worldwide in

Oxford   New York
Auckland   Bangkok   Buenos Aires   Cape Town   Chennai
Dar es Salaam   Delhi   Hong Kong   Istanbul   Karachi   Kolkata
Kuala Lumpur   Madrid   Melbourne   Mexico City   Mumbai
Nairobi   Sao Paulo   Shanghai   Taipei   Tokyo   Toronto

Oxford is a registered trademark of Oxford University Press
in the UK and in certain other countries

Published in India
by Oxford University Press, New Delhi

© Oxford University Press 2001

The moral rights of the author have been asserted
Database right Oxford University Press (maker)

First published 2001
Oxford India Paperbacks 2003

ISBN  0 19 566633 X

Typeset in Dante MT by Eleven Arts, Keshav Puram, Delhi 110 035
Printed by Pauls Press, New Delhi 110 020
Published by Manzar Khan, Oxford University Press
YMCA Library Building, Jai Singh Road, New Delhi 110 001

For Meera

# Contents

# Introduction

## Growing up to write

I grew up in a middle-class Indian family that could afford to give me an education. This enabled me to write and speak in English and exposed me to Western liberal ideas. And so, I found myself in a situation of privilege on the Indian subcontinent. As I grew older I felt it a duty to capture my experiences and articulate them as honestly as I could. My mother taught me that one's life is earned, earned against formidable odds, and one must somehow try to make some sense out of it. Writing, I have discovered, is one way to do it.

I was the eldest son of an engineer who worked for the government in the Punjab. Our family budget was always tight. My mother told us stories from the *Mahabharata* and encouraged in us the virtues of thrift, honesty and responsibility. We lived in the innocence of the Nehruvian age when we still had strong ideals. We believed in socialism, democracy and the UN. We were filled with the excitement of building a nation. Even though the dream soured, Nehru's idealism left a permanent mark on us.

I went to America as a schoolboy for a few years in the 1950s. In my high school I was surprised that we had to attend a class called 'shop', which was filled with lathes, tools and machines, and we learned to work with our hands. We learned to repair a window, make a table or unclog a sink. At the end of the year, we had lost our fear of technology. We had understood Bronowski's dictum that the world is understood through the hand, not the mind—the hand is the cutting edge of the mind. Hence, many Americans become 'tinkerers'. This is a powerful idea for India where we have traditionally had contempt for manual labour. Tinkerers combine knowledge with manual labour, and thus you get innovation. A lack of tinkering may be one of the reasons why we have failed to create an industrial revolution in India.

After completing high school I went on to study philosophy by the banks of the river Charles near Boston at Harvard University. Because American colleges are liberal, I was allowed to experiment with many subjects, and I had the unbelievable luxury of studying Sanskrit with Daniel Ingalls.

After finishing college, I didn't quite know what I wanted to do with my life. I had completed a degree in philosophy, but I had already begun to feel that academic life was stuffy and confining. Philosophy as taught in the Anglo-Saxon world was arid, reduced to linguistic analysis. On the European continent, they did ask the great questions, but the Existentialists were too obscure and too extravagant. Hence, I decided to take 'a year off' from academic work and taste the real world while I decided on a career. Thus, towering with the confidence of twenty, I returned to India. I was lucky to get a marketing job in a company, Richardson Hindustan Ltd, whose chief virtue, it seemed to me, was to let me travel to the towns and villages of India. Soon I began to like the rough-and-tumble of the commercial world, and the academic world grew remote.

I have since lived an active business life, first in Bombay and later in many cities around the world. Most of my life I have been a manager; so, I don't think of myself as a 'literary person'. But I have a passion for the humanities—history, philosophy, art—and a liberal temper that is sceptical of easy and total answers. I also find that I can only live in India, partly because of what I learnt from Cervantes when I lived in Spain. He teaches that glory lies in one's own backyard. The universal, he says, is at odds with the cosmopolitan. The more a man belongs to his own time and space the more he belongs to *all* times and places. I followed Cervantes' advice and I returned to India even when my career dictated otherwise.

Business offered me a lot of action, but it did not provide me enough intellectual stimulation. Hence, I began to keep a diary. Initially my job entailed a great deal of travel to small towns in India, and I had much free time in the evenings in hotels like Sri Krishna Lodge at Ratlam. To pass the time I began to read history. But I was not content to read. I also began to write. Thus, I wrote *Larins Sahib*, which is based on a moment in the history of the Punjab.

All writers, I think, seek continuity between their writing and the life they live. It is a natural thing. Writing needs commitment to a time and place and it brings release from loneliness, which is the human condition. Hence, it is a classic strategy for survival. But it also creates distance between subject and object and the writer risks becoming too much of an observer, uninvolved and unconcerned. He risks becoming self-righteous—a most disagreeable quality—and subjective. By withdrawing from his environment he becomes inauthentic. A writer must always be aware of this risk and remain connected.

Of course, it is common for a writer to stand outside his own culture and be critical—Aristophanes, Euripides, Dante, Shakespeare were passionately and incurably sceptical. But this does not mean that they were adversarial to the ideals of their culture. In fact, they celebrated their culture. It is ironical that the culture that educates us, the patterns of perception learned in our schools is unfriendly to the commercial civilization in which we live. Business people tend to optimism. I am no different and hence, my writing lacks the angst that has been the defining quality of modern literature and theatre. According to 'modern' ethos, an artist should be tormented and die young. He is not expected to create beauty but reveal the sordid truth behind our bourgeois lives. Modern literature and art is hostile to the bourgeois world, although it is financed by uneasy bourgeois money. Indian intellectuals carry the additional burden of having to reinterpret their tradition. Our nineteenth-century thinkers tried to do this either as revivalists or as synthesizers or reformers from Rammohan Roy onwards. Dayanand Saraswathi, Vivekananda, Tagore, Aurobindo—all of them struggled with this task. Today, we don't see intellectuals doing it. Indian writers need to examine our rich, rational tradition and not be swept by the mystical side alone.

## Learning to write

I am comfortable and happy writing in English. If my business discourse can be in English, why not my literary discourse? For me, not unlike others in the Indian middle class, English did not come as a matter of choice. We inherited it from the British Raj. We were sent to English-speaking schools, and as we grew up we found that our command of English was sometimes better than our Hindi or Bengali or any of our mother tongues. Thus, English became one of our many Indian languages. Our mothers knew all along that English was a passport to our futures. Now, with the globalization of the economy, English has become more than ever the language of the world, and our mothers' gamble has paid off. So, as a writer in the twenty-first century I do not have to be apologetic about writing in English, as I did in the late 1960s and 1970s when I wrote these plays. However, although the criticism of those who questioned my right to write in English has diminished, I still feel that there is a problem with writing and performing in English in India.

I have learned to write naturally, as one speaks. In my case, this is the language that middle-class Indians learn in English-medium schools throughout India. It is a national language for all. Indians seem to speak English in pretty much the same way. It is no longer imitative—nostalgic of 'London fogs' or 'Surrey dews'—as it used to be before Independence. It is a nice sounding idiom that has emerged under the bright Indian sun. It is virile and self-confident. Bombay and Delhi set its tone, mainly because they have become the dominant cities of India. Today, it is a flourishing idiom, despite the efforts of many of our politicians to make us forget English.

The English that I speak and write originated with the professional middle class that emerged in the nineteenth century under British rule and the introduction of the English language and western education. This class not only produced clerks for the East India Company, but also lawyers, teachers, engineers, doctors, bureaucrats—all the new professions that were required to run a country. Since passing an exam was the only barrier to entering this class, its members came from various castes and backgrounds. By and large, opportunities were open to all, although the upper castes were the first to seize them. Once they learned English, acquired an education and cleared an exam, rewards and prestige were showered upon them. They became the new elite and they closed ranks.

To my grandfather the English language was a treasured possession. He prided himself on its mastery. I was struck by his strange attachment to a foreign language, but I now realize that it was his window to the world. My uncle used to enjoy pointing out the rich irony of the British teaching us English. It introduced Indian minds to liberal ideas and the ideals of the French Revolution while the British Empire was practising the opposite through colonial rule. Schools and colleges taught liberty and equality, while the British government practised subjugation and inequality. After college, the students from these schools and colleges joined the nationalist movement. By the time my father went to college in the 1930s, there was a thin but growing middle class which had gone through the same education system across India, and had attained a general unity of vision. It had a liberal, humanistic outlook, which was tolerant of ambiguities and shy of certainties. It shared a community of thought, feeling and ideas, and this partly built up a sense of Indian nationality.

It requires a degree of humility to accept nature and evolution. The English language in India is now part of our environment, and we cannot deny it, as we cannot our history. It seems to me that it is just as intrusive to seek to remove English today from India as it was to introduce it during the time of Rammohun Roy and Macaulay. The difference after 150 years is that Indians have become increasingly confident of their English, and this is the English that comes naturally to me.

Aside from naturalness, I also follow the rule of simplicity. If I can use a simpler word, I excise the more difficult one. If I can find a shorter word, I prefer it to a longer one. If I can make a sentence of five words, I prefer it to one with seven words. This leads to rework, but it also results in brevity, and there is nobility in brevity. Reworking isn't fun, but it does feel good when the manuscript gets better and better. In the end, my writing is functional, I expect. It is not ambitious—but then, I have neither the talent nor the inclination to experiment with language and form.

I taught myself to write with a tiny, 85-page paperback called *The Elements of Style* by Strunk and White.[1] As far as I know there is no better book on writing English, and astonishing for a composition rulebook, it made the *New York Times* bestseller list in 1962 and has stayed there for years. I write by ear, often with difficulty and seldom with an exact notion of grammar, but it hasn't put me off this book. Blaise Pascal agrees with being natural: 'when we come across a natural style, we are surprised and delighted; for we expected an author and we find a man.'

## Writing for the theatre

Writing a play takes a certain amount of audacity, which I seem to lack today. I wrote all my plays in my twenties. I had more courage then and

I would be very scared of writing a play now. Theatre audiences are very critical. One mistake and you are through. Readers of books are, I think, far more sympathetic. To write for the theatre you have to *know* the theatre. Ideally, you should have been an actor or a director, at least for a short while, and hang around the theatre a lot. To publish a book you don't have to know about publishing and printing in the same way. For a person of the theatre, performance is the thing. On the stage it is always *here* and *now*. A play is not on paper. It is there to share with actors, directors, set designers, electricians and music makers. Once it is written, I usually try to stay away from the stage because I am not a 'theatre person'. I find I am often uncomfortable with theatre people and actors, who in some cases, are on the stage all the time.

Theatre's business is to entertain people. Nothing needs less justification than successful entertainment. People pay hard-earned money to buy a ticket, and they must be given pleasure. Aristotle demanded that even tragedy should first entertain. The problem for a playwright is that the art is so utterly dependent upon stage production and the intervention of the actor.

After these three plays I wrote a novel, *A Fine Family* (Penguin), and I learned a great deal about the difference between the two genres. A novel is generally written in the past tense. It is the past reported in the present. In drama, it is always now. This gives theatre an energy and vitality, which the novelist longs for in his work. A play is what happens. A novel is what one person tells us about what happened. In the end, I think there are more similarities than differences between novels and plays for both interpret life. Life as it appears to us in our daily experience is an unintelligible chaos of happenings. Life as it occurs is senseless. Both novelists and playwrights pick out the significant incidents from the chaos of daily happiness, and arrange them so that their relation to one another becomes significant, thus changing us from bewildered readers or spectators of a monstrous confusion to persons conscious of life and meaning. Time is an important ally in this. Henri Bergson once said that the great advantage of time is that it prevents everything from happening at once.

If I had to go back and write these plays all over again, I would have insisted on working with a group of actors as soon as I had the first draft of the play. I would have given lots of room to actors to improvise upon and I would have trained myself to be receptive to what was working on the stage and what was not. I would have learned 'to listen' and 'to see' what an audience sees and a writer does not. I would have learned to be humble and learn from the actors and their improvisational exercises. I realize it is a different kind of work for a writer to write in this manner when he is so used to working alone, but it cannot be helped. The test of a play is how it works on the stage and not how it reads.

## Writing *Larins Sahib*

I began to think of *Larins Sahib* during my travels in the bazaars of the Punjab when I was learning to sell Vicks Vaporub at the age of twenty-four. I was reading at the time a history of the Punjab, in which I came across the unusual Lawrence brothers. Henry Lawrence was the most interesting and the least imperial. His brother, George, was a soldier in the North-west and John was an empire builder who went on to become Lord Lawrence, the Governor-General and Viceroy of India. We called him 'Tunda Lat' because his statue in the Lawrence Gardens in Lahore lacked an arm. Henry was unusual because he formed easy friendships with the Sikh noble families. I was particularly fascinated by his warm and affectionate relationship with Sher Singh, the scion of the Attari family; the fiery Rani Jindan, the widow of Ranjit Singh, and her son Duleep, who was taken away from her when he was young and who became the tragic 'black prince' at Queen Victoria's court. I don't quite know why I thought of it as a play. It could have been a novel. But it was great fun doing research over the next twelve months. Reading the history of Punjab was for me also a search for identity. I was drawn to the events in 1846 because that is when the British first arrived in the Punjab, and the first reactions of the Punjabis to the English, and vice versa, determined how we would behave for a hundred years thereafter.

The events in the play take place in the confused period in the Punjab after the death of Maharaja Ranjit Singh in 1839. Ranjit Singh had established over forty years an empire in the northwest India on the ruins of the Mughal Empire. It was a large territory between the river Sutlej and the Himalayan mountain ranges of Ladakh, Karakoram, Hindukush and Sulaiman. On today's map it would have covered Indian and Pakistan Punjab, the Northwest Frontier province, and Jammu and Kashmir. A European traveller, Baron C. Von Hugel, called the empire 'the most wonderful object in the whole world'.[2] Other contemporaries compared Ranjit Singh to Bonaparte. A French traveller referred to the one-eyed Sikh as 'a miniature Napoleon'. The British agreed that both were 'men of military genius'. The Sikh monarchy was 'Napoleonic in the suddenness of its rise, the brilliancy of its success, and the completeness of its overthrow'.[3] The British took over his empire within ten years of his death. The comparison was also apt because of Ranjit Singh's enthusiasm for employing distinguished former Napoleonic officers. Generals Avitable and Ventura, Colonels Court and Allard and many others helped make his army into an efficient machine—as effective as that of the East India Company.

While Ranjit Singh was alive, both sides had sufficient regard for each other's capabilities to avoid a head-on clash. But after his death, the Sikh kingdom was plunged into chaos. He had too many wives and too many successors, and as rival court factions sought support for their preferred candidates, the authority drained back to the army. The British saw their chance and the inevitable collision took place late in 1845. The first Sikh War began with two ferocious battles in the vicinity of Ferozepur. Helped by the treachery of the Sikh courtiers and Commanders, who betrayed their own army, the British grabbed a victory from the jaws of defeat at Sobraon, a costly battle in which the Sikhs lost 10,000 men and the British 2400.

It was a sobering result and the British ruled out a more expensive bid for Lahore and opted for a peace package consisting of indemnity, partial annexation, a reduction in the Sikh army and other safeguards. The annexation brought them some territory in the Punjab and their frontier moved from the Sutlej to the Beas river. Since the Sikhs could not pay the full indemnity, the British took Kashmir instead and the vast Himalayan country between the Beas and the Indus rivers. Foolishly, they sold it to Gulab Singh, the Dogra Raja of Jammu, who had been one of Ranjit Singh's feudatories, and who now became a vassal of the British. Thus the princely state of Jammu and Kashmir was formed, which would descend through the Hindu king's successors until 1947 and become a source of contention between India and Pakistan. No one thought twice at the time about the fact that a Hindu king would rule had over a predominantly Muslim people, just as Muslim nawabs ruled over Hindu populations in Awadh, Hyderabad and elsewhere. But Kashmir would enjoy a century of peace and prosperity that it seldom saw before or after.

After the first Sikh War, the British left behind an active and unusual resident, Henry Lawrence with a small staff and some British troops. His job was to uphold and direct the Regency Council, which would now operate in the name of Dalip Singh, Ranjit Singh's minor son. The resident was to see to it that the Sikh court and council would hold their own against the restless Sikh army and especially the disgruntled troops, who had been betrayed by their leaders and then laid off by the treaty. In 1848, the Maharaja's garrison in the southern city of Multan mutinied and killed two Englishmen. This was precisely the opportunity that Lord Dalhousie, the new governor-general needed. As the mutiny spread among the Sikh troops to the rest of Punjab, a large British army crossed the Sutlej once again from Ferozepur, passed the Ravi and the Chenab, and fought a major battle at Chillanwalla on the Jhelum. The Sikhs hailed it a victory, but the British pretended otherwise—even though they had lost 3000 men. However, the British came back a month later and decisively won the battle of Gujarat, and with it the prize of Punjab. 'On 29 March 1849, Maharaja Dalip Singh held his court for the last time in his life to sign the document of annexation in Roman letters and to become a pensioner of the British. The "majestic fabric," raised by Maharaja Ranjit Singh was a thing of the past'.[4]

This is the historic background to the play. After writing two acts, I discovered that the Theatre Group in Bombay had announced a playwriting contest with a prize of Rs 10,000 (which was a lot of money in 1968) and an offer to stage the winning play. This was just the incentive that I needed to finish the play. I entered it for the competition and fidgeted for three months. *Larins Sahib* won from among eighty entries, many of them from established authors. Theatre Group's production opened in 1969 in Bombay, directed by Deryck Jefferies with Zul Vellani as Lawrence and Roger Pereira as Sher Singh. Many productions followed, including one at Lawrence School, Sanawar, directed by Feroza Das. My favourite was the one in 1990 by Rahul da Cunha (the son of Gerson, who had been on the jury of the Sultan Padamsee prize in 1968) with Tom Alter as Lawrence, Rajat Kapur as Sher Shah and Nisha Singh as Rani Jindan. I think it worked well because the director allowed the actors to improvise and turn some of the lines of the Sikhs into Punjabi. Thus, it got over some of the problems of performing in English. The audiences in Bombay loved it, and the company travelled with it to the Edinburg festival where they performed it on the fringe. I learned from watching this production that for English theatre to work on the stage in India, it needed to be 'Indianized'. This doesn't mean that the play has to be in Hinglish *a la* Zee television, but the audience clearly needs familiar signals from the actor, in the way they speak and their body language to help them identify with the characters.

*Larins Sahib*, in the end, is a work of youth. It betrays a degree of diffidence and it could certainly be improved upon. If I had to go back to it, I would work on Lawrence's motivation. I would try to explain why such a fine person with ideals crumbles so easily. Hubris explains it only partially. When Oxford University Press offered to publish this volume, I was tempted to go back and work on the problem of 'the three avatars of Henry Lawrence' as M.K.Naik of Karnatak University calls them.[5] These are the: enlightened empire-builder, the would-be 'Lion of the Punjab' and the cog in the wheel of the East India Company. Naik thinks, with some justification, that the three are not well integrated. It goes back, I think, to the same problem of motivation. Perhaps I am too lazy, or it is too far in the past, or it is drained out of my system, but the fact is that I did not return to the play. Hence, this remains a challenge for the next director and the cast. I would encourage them not only to improvise with the sound of the language but also to try to correct this flaw as much as possible in the performance.

## Writing *Mira*

Saints come naturally to Indians, and one of the reasons certainly is the influence of bhakti poets like Mira. I grew up in a bhakti-filled atmosphere. My father was a mystic and my mother used to sing Mira's devotional songs in the mornings. But I had received a secular and liberal education, acquired a sceptical temper, and I found saints deeply problematic. I did not dismiss spiritual experience, but it would take a great deal to make me a believer. In my twenties I began to question what it meant to be a saint, and this led me to write *Mira*.

Indians believe in three basic ideas: first, the world is sorrow (*dukha*) and suffering is at the root of existence. This idea has come to us from the Buddha. The second is the notion that our day-to-day world is an illusion, and we must transcend it to find *reality*. Shankara (AD 788–820) expressed this notion must forcefully. The third is the passionate belief that I or my soul can become one with God through unconditional love and devotion. This is the central idea of bhakti. Love has long been a metaphor for religious experience in India. An ancient passage in the *Brihadaranyaka Upanishad* compares the attainment of freedom and enlightenment to the experience of a man in his wife's embrace. A person, it says, 'in the embrace of the intelligent Soul [knows] nothing within or without…[H]is desire is satisfied, in which the soul is his desire, in which he is without desire and without sorrow'.[6] Tamil saints first popularized this idea of bhakti, and later it was spread across India after AD 1400 by a galaxy of medieval bhakti saints—Kabir, Mira, Nanak, Tulsidas, Lalla, Chaitanya, Tukaram, Ravidas and many others.

The chief mood of bhakti poetry is erotic (*sringara*), as seen from a woman's point of view, whether in its phase of separation or of union. When Mira addresses love poems to Krishna she adopts the feminine personae of a wife, an illicit lover, a woman with a tryst, even Radha herself. Krishna is her god but he is also her lover. The most common sentiment is the pain of separation from the lover and the constant theme is self-surrender of the beloved.

In classical times Indians sensibly pursued multiple ends in life. These were:—virtue or righteousness (*dharma*), wealth and power (*artha*), pleasure and sex (*kama*), and release or enlightenment (*moksha*). During the prime of life a worldly householder (*grihasta*) pursued wealth, power and pleasure. Only later in life did he turn to *moksha*. Thus, in antiquity there was a nice balance in the aims of life and Indian civilization was not as 'other-worldly' as it became later in the medieval times when a fifth objective (*pancham purushartha*) swept the minds and hearts of men and women. This was love and it supplanted all other goals, becoming the highest, higher even than *moksha*.

By reaching out to the masses in their everyday languages, the bhakti saints created a veritable social revolution. By offering entry to the lower castes they forced reform on Hinduism and prevented mass conversion to Islam. Since boundless love of God was the only requirement all were rendered equal. By promoting a direct relationship between the soul and God, the bhakti saints eliminated the priests (as Martin Luther did in the Reformation and Buddha did two thousand years earlier). They offered confidence to the poor masses and helped bind together the diverse elements of the subcontinent into a single functioning society. A new form of musical composition also took shape in their songs, which continues to be performed even today in concerts, and on the radio and television.

Although saints like Mira subverted the traditional ideals of Indian womanhood and challenged the social order, her mystical love for Krishna did not create the sort of problems for her as Saint Joan's visions did in the West. The conservative Rajputs thought she was mad, or a liar or a sorceress but she was not burned at the stake as Joan was.

It is curious that romantic love arose in medieval West at the same time. Medieval Western society was also rigid and arranged marriages were the norm. Whereas in Europe romantic love went on to become a worldly norm, in India bhakti was absorbed into the reform movements of the nineteenth century and remained an otherworldly phenomena. Only later in Hindi cinema, from the 1940s, did romantic love begin to spill out into this world and the secular life.

Critics contend that bhakti flowered because Muslim rule prevented most men from pursuing worldly power. Society had become more rigid, the caste system more entrenched, which checked the ambitions and mobility of men. Turning inwards was a natural response, allowing people to accept their unhappy material condition. They argue that bhakti permanently damaged the Indian psyche by making us ambivalent about the value of human action in this world, and this places us at a competitive disadvantage today. Personally, I am wary of such cultural explanations. I do believe, however, that whether one is a believer or an agnostic, these desperate medieval lovers made a great contribution to world civilization, and traditions like bhakti provide us today with a safeguard against the onslaught of the mindless global culture.

Historians differ with regard to the date of Mira's birth, marriage, and death.[7] But all agree that she was a princess of the Rathore clan of Merta in Rajasthan. According to the most reliable account, Mira was born in AD 1498 when the Muslim dynasty of the Lodhis ruled in Delhi. Another Muslim king, Bahadur Shah, ruled Gujarat to the south. It was during Mira's lifetime—in 1526 to be exact—that Babur, the first great Mughal, invaded India, and established the Mughal dynasty at Delhi, and it dominated India for two hundred years. Thus, Mira lived in a time of exceeding political turmoil. Muslims and Hindus were constantly at war and there were bloody conflicts amongst the Rajputs themselves. Mira must have known frequent deaths amongst her Rajput relatives, whose first imperative was to maintain high traditions of martial valour and family honour. Rajput honour required courage in men, and chastity and obedience in women in an archetypal feudal patriarchy, whose extreme form was the custom of *jauhar*, in which women avoided falling into the hands of the enemy after a defeat by committing mass suicide in a fire.

Mira's great-grandfather, it seems, was the famous Rathore noble Raja Jodhaji, the founder of Jodhpur. She grew up in the company of her cousin Jaimal who would become a hero in Rajput history. She married the son and heir-apparent of the great Rana Sangha, head of the Sisodiya clan and the ruler of Mewar, who was the unquestioned leader of the Rajputs at the time, and ruled from the famed citadel, Chittor. Thus, she entered a state of unquestioning duty, heavy marital responsibility, and a rigid domestic hierarchy. It is not quite clear when Mira abandoned the palace altogether to begin the life of a wandering singer. Perhaps the important turning point was the bloody battle of Khanua in 1527, when the Mughals defeated the Rajput confederacy under the leadership of Mewar.

There are rich legends that attempt to explain Mira's conversion. One says that she refused to perform the first duty of a new daughter-in-law, which is to worship the family deity, the goddess Kali or Durga. Her obvious absorption in something other than her marriage bed is said to have aroused the suspicions of her husband who burst into her room one day hoping to surprise her in adultery. But he found her deep in worship before the idol of Krishna. Another legend tells of a wedding being celebrated in the house next door when she was a child. As the excitement grew in anticipation of the groom's arrival, Mira asked her mother about her own bridegroom. Her mother laughed and pointed to Krishna's statuette, saying, 'There he is, your bridegroom.' They say that the Sisodiyas sent her a cup of poison, which turned into ambrosia. A venomous snake was put into her basket to kill her. The snake turned into a garland of flowers.

In the end, Mira struck a radical blow at nearly everything that constituted the feudal conventions of the Rajput aristocracy, and the mighty Sisodiyas of Chittor felt shamed by her public defiance. Hence, it didn't come as a surprise to me that in Rajasthan her name was often used as a term of abuse for promiscuous women. By abandoning her husband, she had defied male prerogative and upset Rajput honour. The Rajputs in turn had retaliated and suppressed her name not only in written records but deep within society's memory as well. Her devotional songs, so popular all over the country, were not sung in Rajasthan until recently.[8]

Since Mira was forgotten in Rajasthan, scholars tell us that the mercantile middle class in Gujarat preserved her memory over the centuries and this was linked to the rise of the weaving communities. It was Mahatma Gandhi who resuscitated her in the twentieth century when he entered the freedom movement in 1915. Through his writings, political speeches and his prayer meetings Mira entered the national consciousness. Gandhi had wisely tapped a reservoir of goodwill for bhakti in the Indian psyche and secured for Mira a wide popular base amongst the Indian middle and lower classes and a place in the nationalist political culture. Following his example, Tagore named his daughter after Mira. So did many others.

Mira's poems are an outpouring of love and faith. No one hearing them sung can doubt for a moment the intensity and genuineness of her mystical faith. As a Rajput princess, she gave up the security of a palace and a husband, and took to wandering, singing and dancing—a most courageous and extreme step for any woman to take in any society. The problem for the playwright is how to describe this transformation from a woman into a saint. And how does one begin to explain the immense faith of a devotee? Saints are not interesting for the theatre. Only human beings are. God is ultimately a human problem, a human endeavour by finite beings to overcome their incompleteness. Thus, a longing for completeness is the starting-point of this lovesick, mystical way. And how does one describe the relation between the seeker and the transcendent something else in relation to which the world is flattened? Mira's poems suggest that the heart feels Him to be present when it feels His absence most keenly.

To solve these problems I imagined Mira as a high-spirited young bride, who comes and shatters the emotionally charged atmosphere of formality in sixteen century Mewar, a state much burdened by a sense of its historical destiny. I focused on the evolving relationship between a husband and wife. Initially, there is novelty; the embarrassment of two young people discovering each other in the typical Indian situation where physical touch precedes emotional contact. As the novelty wears, the Rana becomes absorbed in the affairs of the state and the imminent war with the Mughal. And Mira feels the frustration of a wife whose husband is not available. Mira's demands too, both sexual and emotional, seem to be greater. Her love is big. She naively runs after him, and he withdraws further. As she discovers that her husband is not equal to her love, she becomes disillusioned with marriage.

Added to this is the failure of not having a son. She wonders if she has let her husband down in not giving him an heir. She becomes victim to a palace rumour that she is barren. She despairs. In her vulnerability she almost succumbs to her cousin Jai, who secretly loves her and is one of the few who understands her. At this point she turns to her personal god, Krishna, the dark erotic god of love, and entreats him to give her a son—a natural thing for a lonely woman to do in order to win her husband back. Soon she finds, however, that she is transferring her love to the image and has become victim to a new attachment. The Rana, unable to understand her preoccupation with Krishna, thinks that she has a lover. But he soon discovers that he is wrong and believes that she is going mad. The others think this strange behaviour may be a result of her barrenness—perhaps she is possessed.

Mira's battle to master her insane attachment to her god and her eventual realization that she can master it, constitute a fulfilment. In her mastery is her sainthood. From a reality in itself, the image of Krishna has become a symbol of a greater reality beyond her. At last she is at peace with herself but detached from the phenomenal world. This then is the inner logic for the transformation of a human being into a love-obsessed bhakti saint. I am not quite sure that it works entirely. After all, there are many neglected, barren wives who do not become saints. But at least it is an attempt at an explanation. Most renderings of the Mira story don't even make an attempt—they just assume that she was born a saint, which I find unsatisfactory. The other theme that I have explored is the tragedy of her husband who has to suffer the pain and misery of this transformation—the price he has to pay, so to speak, so that she can become a saint.

While *Larins Sahib* was in the genre of the 'well made play', *Mira* could only succeed as non-natural theatre with lots of song and dance. But I had little experience with theatre craft and for months I struggled with this problem. Then, one day my company transferred me to the head office in New York. This was in 1969 when Grotowski was the rage and New Yorkers were mesmerized by his concept of 'total theatre'. The city abounded with experimental groups. One of these was La Mama, under the able leadership of Ellen Stewart. The enormously successful rock musical, *Hair*, had started there. I was completed transported by the possibilities that had suddenly opened up for my second play. (Tragically, I was at the time ignorant of our own theatrical traditions; only later did I discover that 'total theatre' had existed in India for centuries in the tamasha of Maharashtra, the Yakshagana of Mysore, the Bhawai of Gujarat, the jatra of Bengal.)

When Ellen Stewart accepted my first, inadequate draft of *Mira*, I could not believe it. It needed a young Martin Brenzell of La Mama to intoduce me to the magic of theatre—to teach me that theatre could be created minimally with body movements of the actors. Since naturalistic dialogue was out of the question, I began to conceive of *Mira* as ritualistic theatre and I began to re-write the play using aphoristic dialogue. Martin Brenzell found equity actors who had been trained by Martha Graham and could also sing. David Walker wrote the music for two musicians and soon we were in business.

Directors do not like playwrights interfering with productions. Brenzell's solution was to hold rehearsals from midnight to five in the morning. Since I had a regular nine to five job, this turned out to be an effective strategy. Occasionally, we would meet at 3 p.m. for breakfast (yes, for breakfast!) at his favourite café in the East Village and he would fill me in on the progress of the production. Nevertheless, I did go to a few rehearsals and each time I left enthralled. The entire play had been set to music and dance. All the actors were on stage all the time and they made beautiful pictures with their bodies. When Mira said, 'I am an ant on a matchstick bit at both ends,' the actors made such a picture with their bodies. The problem was that Brenzell was never satisfied and he would change the picture every night. The actors complained that they felt they were rehearsing a new play every night right up to opening night. In the end, Brenzell's was an exciting interpretation. Clive Barnes of the *New York Times* gave it a rave review, and I felt a few inches taller.

There have been many productions since, including Alyque Padamsee's visual enactment in Bombay with backward and forward projected slides. It was stylish but static. There was even a production in Spanish with a lovely translation by Enrique Hett that was published by the Instito Nacional de Bellas Artes. M.K. Raina's production with Jawahar Wattle's music brought back some of the energy, but none equalled the glory of the La Mama production.

## On 9 *Jakhoo Hill*

After writing two plays based on historic personages, I thought that I would turn to contemporary concerns. Hence, my next play is set in recent times. On one level *9 Jakhoo Hill* is about the changing order— the old middle class giving way to the new. Ansuya and her family belong to the old class and Deepak and Chitra to the new. Although this change had begun in the India of the 1960s, when the play is set, it accelerated in the 1980s and 1990s; hence the play resonated with audiences when it was performed in the mid-nineties and continues to be relevant today.

The most striking feature of contemporary India is the rise of a confident new middle class, which is full of energy and drive and is making things happen. That it goes about it in an uninhibited and amoral fashion is also true. It is different from the older bourgeoisie, which was leisurely, tolerant and ambiguous. The new class is street smart; it has had to fight to rise from the bottom and it has learnt to manoeuvre the system. It is easy to despair over its vulgarity, its new-rich mentality and its lack of education. But whether India can deliver the goods depends a great deal on it.

The old middle class, consisting of people like my grandfather and father, first emerged in the nineteen century with the spread of English education. It produced the professionals who stepped into the shoes of the departing English in 1947 and have for long monopolized the rewards of our society. Its chief virtue was that it was based on education and merit with relatively free entry, but it was also a class alienated from the mass of the people and unsure of its identity. The new middle class, on the other hand, is based on money, drive and an ability to get things done. Whereas the old class was liberal, idealistic and inhibited, the new order is pragmatic and refreshingly free from colonial hang-ups.

My father, like other members of the old class, seemed to lead two separate lives, neatly divided into two compartments. During the day at work he wore western clothes, spoke English, and followed the rational, individualistic life of an official of the British Raj. In the evening he wore a loose-fitting kurta, spoke Punjabi, ate Indian food, listened to Indian music and meditated like a good Hindu. Years later I heard the expression, 'cultural commuter', which I think fitted my father and his generation quite well, although it does not capture the price they must have paid in the sense of disorientation and alienation that they experienced.

We may feel regret at the eclipse of the old bourgeoisie, especially because it possessed the unique characteristic of being a class based on free entry, education and capability. We may feel equally uneasy that a new class based on money is replacing it. However, this is not a new phenomenon. It has happened repeatedly in all societies, particularly after the advent of the industrial revolution. When India became independent, the middle class was tiny—around five per cent of the population—but we had a clear idea of what our parents wanted us to grow up to be. They wanted us to be nice Indian boys, well-bred, handsome, intelligent and good at games. We were groomed to be brown sahibs, the rightful rulers of free India. They tried to educate us in private schools because the government schools were bad. Those who could afford it sent theirs to Doon and Mayo (even when it pinched their pockets). We became good at cricket and tennis and adequate at studies. 'He is a good all-rounder,' was the model held up before us. After school, we went on to Delhi's St Stephen College or Presidency College in Calcutta and Madras. A few lucky ones even managed to go Oxford and Cambridge. We were expected to acquire the basic intellectual equipment at the university, but not to become scholars. From the 1960s, the path became more competitive and those who could get in chose technical and managerial institutions—the IITs and IIMs.

After college, we were ready to join the IAS or industry or the professions—all the pleasant niches for which the older Indian bourgeoisie groomed its young. With secure jobs in our pockets, we were married off to good middle-or upper middle-class girls whom we courted in the Gymkhana clubs and at hill-stations during our summer holidays. We were ready to become pillars of the establishment and repeat the process with our young. As we prospered in our jobs, we built houses in South Delhi and went to stylish parties where we met our friends, rubbed shoulders with diplomats and enjoyed the wit of the intellectual elite of our land. Could one have a better recipe for the enviably happy life? We had fulfilled the dreams of our fathers. But why then, with all our advantages, do we feel a gnawing pain in the gut?

We are Macaulay's children, not Manu's. Our ambivalence goes back to that day when Macaulay persuaded the British government to teach English to Indians. Our position is similar to Rammohun Roy's, who had two houses in Calcutta. One was his 'Bengali house' and the other his 'European house'. In the Bengali house he lived with his wife and children in the traditional Indian way. The 'European house', on the other hand, was tastefully done up with English furniture and was used to entertain his European friends. Someone teased him by saying that everything in the Bengali house is Bengali except Rammohun Roy; and everything in the European house is European except Rammohan Roy. The dilemma of today's 'brown sahib' is similar. We can live our hypocritical lives only for so long; ultimately we must question our recipe for the enviably happy life. Our inner lives are a parody. We have one foot in India, the other in the West, and we belong to neither culture. Rai Saheb is a caricature of this class, but even the sensitive Karan Chand, who is aware of this problem, is a victim.

*9 Jakhoo Hill* is about many things. Aside from the changing order, it is about the hold of Indian mothers on their sons, about a fading class clinging foolishly to spent dreams, about the incestuous obsessions of ageing uncles. But the main theme is the betrayal of sexual love. Traditional Indian social life is fundamentally incomprehensible to the West largely because we Indians have always regarded sexual passion as a relatively trivial matter. As a result we set higher value upon filial rather than marital love. The Indian male appears to western eyes as effeminate and a 'mama's boy' because he often gives precedence to his mother over his wife. The 'modern' Indian male, however, is caught in a dilemma. Modernity demands of him that he think of sexual love as a chief source of virtue. He is thus in a dilemma of conflicting values between his 'traditional' duty to his mother and his 'modern' duty to his wife. Generally he tends to make a mess of both and a fool of himself in the bargain.

I set the play in Simla because I grew up there in the 1950s and was familiar with its society. I had seen or heard talk of Rai Sahebs and Amritas throughout my childhood. In time, I set it during the Diwali of 1962 when the country was at war with China. I think this was a great turning point—the war ended our age of innocence and shattered our Nehruvian dreams. Nehru died soon afterwards and our society also began to change. With the coming of Indira Gandhi values began to depart from our political life and governance became immoral. A new personalized style of politics came into being. Institutions started to erode especially the Congress Party.

As the play opens, Ansuya's family, which has seen better times before the partition of the country, broods over the old days. They are being forced to sell their house to pay off their debts. Ever since her father died, her uncle Karan has been Ansuya's companion. The noble beauty of his mind draws him to her and they share an idyllic life of books. For Karan too Ansuya's family is the only one he has known. He is a professor, more comfortable with thought than action. He has not been a success in the eyes of the world and has reached the twilight when hopes are fast beginning to fade and life is becoming a constant looking back. He needs his niece more than he realizes but is unwilling to admit his excessive interest in her. She is aware of his feelings towards her and they occasionally bother her. But Ansuya is really troubled by her static, decaying, mental existence. She yearns for the city where people *do* things. She feels stifled by her closed life and the incestuous elite that makes up Simla's society. Into this quiet, desperate idleness comes Deepak, full of energy and ambition, and infects everyone.

This play lay in a drawer, gathering dust for twenty years. When I moved to Delhi in the mid-nineties, I gave it to Bhaskar Ghose, who saw something in it and persuaded the Yatrik troupe to perform it. We held a series of readings and I realized that it needed a fair amount of work. After that it became a sort of collaboration between the Yatrik cast and myself. I gave them the room to improvise and they returned the compliment, and I think the play improved.

## Notes

1. William Strunk and E.B. White, *The Elements of Style*, New York, 1979.
2. Hugel, Baron C. Von, *Travels in Kashmir and the Punjab*, London, 1845, p. 293.
3. Lepel Griffin, *Ranjit Singh and the Sikh Barrier between Our Growing Empire and Central Asia*, Oxford, 1905, pp. 9–10.
4. J.S. Grewal, *The Sikhs of the Punjab*, part 2, vol. 3, *New Cambridge History of India* (ed. Johnson, G. et al), Cambridge, 1990, p.127.
5. M.K.Naik, 'The Three Avatars of Henry Lawrence: A Study of Gurcharan Das' *Larins Sahib*', in *The Literary Criterion*, (ed. C.D. Narasimhaiah), vol. xii, nos. 2 & 3, Mysore 1976.
6. Hume, *The Thirteen Principal Upanishads*, 1931, p.136
7. Priyadas' commentary on Nabhadas' *Bhaktamal*, written in AD 1712, has shaped the historical work on Mirabai. There is only one indisputably known fact that is linked with her name. Namely, that as a woman, Mira spurned her caste and family obligations in order to live out a life with Krishna. Nabhadas began his entry on Mira in the *Bhaktamal* by saying that Mira left her clan (*kul*) and society and all notions of decorum in order to worship Krishna. Priyadas' account of Mira provided two other details, which were missing in Nabhadas. One was the fact that she was born in Merta; the other that she was married to the Rana of Chittor. Priyadas then recounted

Mira's refusal to pay obeisance to the Sisodiya goddess (*kuladevi*). See Parita Mukta, *Upholding the Common Life: The Community of Mirabai*, Delhi, 1997. It is the best scholarly attempt to come to grips with the biographical material on Mirabai.

8. Parita Mukta has confirmed this in her book.

# Larins Sahib

*Larins Sahib* won the Sultan Padamsee Prize in 1968, offered by the Theatre Group, Bombay. It was first produced by Deryck Jeffereis at the Bhulabhai Theatre, Bombay in July 1969, with the following cast:

| | |
|---|---|
| Henry Hardinge | Anthony Dale |
| Fredrick Currie | Bomi Kapadia |
| H.M. Elliot | Keith Stevenson |
| Henry Lawrence | Zul Vellani |
| Sher Singh | Roger C.B. Pereira |
| Dalip Singh | Ranjit Chowdhry |
| Baba | Minoo Chhoi |
| Rani Jindan Kaur | Farida Sonavala |
| Sardar Lal Singh | Bell deSouza |
| Sardar Tej Singh | Francis A. Menezes |
| Lt. Herbert Edwardes | Cyrus Bharucha |
| Capt. James Abbot | Homi Mulla |
| Lt. Harry Lumsden | Yohan Jeffereis |

'Go out', said the Hero-makers
and the men behind them. 'Be
another Henry Lawrence. Do
your duty . . . and if necessary die . . .'

MICHAEL EDWARDES, *The Necessary Hell*

# Characters

*[In order of appearance]*

| | |
|---|---|
| HENRY HARDINGE | the Governor-General |
| FREDERICK CURRIE | the Foreign Secretary |
| H.M. ELLIOT | Secretary to the Governor-General's Council |
| HENRY LAWRENCE | |
| SHER SINGH: | |
| DALIP SINGH | the Maharaja of Punjab |
| BABA | Dalip's old servant |
| RANI JINDAN KAUR | the Regent |
| SARDAR LAL SINGH | the Wazir |
| SARDAR TEJ SINGH | the Commander-in-Chief of the Khalsa |
| LT. HERBERT EDWARDES | |
| CAPT. JAMES ABBOT | } Lawrence's 'famous young men' |
| LT. HARRY LUMSDEN | |

FIRST SENTRY, SECOND SENTRY, OLD WOMAN, FIRST BRAHMIN, SECOND BRAHMIN, PROSECUTOR, YOUNG WIDOW, COURT HERALD, ROYAL ADC, PUNKAH COOLIES, SEPOY, COURTIERS, CROWD

*The action of the play takes place mostly in and around Lahore, and briefly in Calcutta, in the year 1846*

# Act One Scene I

The Governor-General's camp on the banks of the Sutlej, halfway between Lahore and Delhi. It is 20 March 1846, a month after the battle of Sobraon, better known as the First Sikh War. Hardinge, Currie and Elliot are present inside a tent. A half hidden coolie is drowsily pulling the cord of the swaying punkah. In the far right-hand corner are a number of hammock-like chairs with arm-pieces to rest weary legs. They have an attachment screwed on to the right arm-piece which swings out to hold a glass. Hardinge has a glass of brandy in one hand and a cigar in another. Currie and Elliot look on solicitously.

HARDINGE:    Where the devil is Lawrence?

ELLIOT:    He should be here any minute, sir.

HARDINGE:    What the devil is the time?

ELLIOT:    Eleven o'clock, sir.

HARDINGE:    Currie, what about the Peshawar despatch?

CURRIE:    Yes, it's come in, sir. I am afraid, sir, there's . . .

HARDINGE:    (*Interrupting.*) *Koi hai?*

ELLIOT:    I'll get it, sir.
        (*Replaces Hardinge's glass.*)

HARDINGE:    Yes, carry on, Currie.

CURRIE:    I am afraid there's bad news, sir.

HARDINGE:    What?

CURRIE:    From the border.

HARDINGE:    Which one?

CURRIE:    Frontier, sir. Peshawar.

HARDINGE:    Oh!
    (*Pause.*)
    Damn these bloody tribes! Damn this bloody country. Damn the whole world . . .
    (*Pause.*)
    This brandy's no good.

ELLIOT:    It's recently come in from London, sir. Travellers.'

HARDINGE:    It's the devilish air then. Everything in India is second-rate.
    Even travellers' best becomes second-rate in India.

CURRIE:   Even the men become second-class in India, sir.

HARDINGE:   What sort of a bloke is Lawrence?

ELLIOT:   Never seen him myself. But I'm told he's quite a character.

CURRIE:   One can hardly credit what one sees, sir.

   (*Mockingly.*)

He is practically a native. If I may say so sir, I think his younger brother, John, is more the sort of person you need for this job.

HARDINGE:   How many Lawrences *are* there in the Punjab?

ELLIOT:   Three, sir.

HARDINGE:   Good God! Who's *the* Lawrence of the Punjab?

ELLIOT:   Henry, I believe, sir.

HARDINGE:   Are you sure?

ELLIOT:   Yes, sir.

HARDINGE:   Damn it, we don't want the wrong man. Who's this younger one—what's his name?

CURRIE:   John, sir.

HARDINGE:   Why is he better?

CURRIE:   He's a regular sort, you know. Civil servant, Haileybury, efficient, proven record, very Christian, proper, doesn't mix with the natives . . .

HARDINGE:   (*Interrupting.*) What makes you think we need a 'regular sort?'

CURRIE:   (*Confused.*) Well, well . . . ah, we always need regular sorts.

HARDINGE:   What do *you* think, Elliot?

ELLIOT:   Well sir, the reputation of this man is phenomenal.

HARDINGE:   Which man, Elliot?

ELLIOT:   Henry, sir.

HARDINGE:   (*Shortly.*) Good God, which one is Henry?

ELLIOT:   *The* Lawrence, sir.

HARDINGE:   Quite, quite. Now Elliot, you were saying?

ELLIOT:   I was saying, sir, that this man has built a phenomenal reputation. Just two years on the border as a minor clerk with the Revenue Survey, and he's become a legend. I believe he's on first-name terms with most of the nobility of the Punjab. They swear by him, and the peasantry of the Ferozepur district think he's some kind of a saviour.

HARDINGE:   Is he a soldier?

ELLIOT:   Yes, sir.

HARDINGE:   What's his rank?

ELLIOT:   Major, sir. But he's been due a promotion for some time.

CURRIE:   Precisely, sir. You can't appoint such a junior man to this post. Why, you'll be superseding half the British Army and alienating the whole British establishment.

HARDINGE:   Hang the British establishment!

(*Lawrence enters. He is forty years old, but looks younger, has a long, brooding face, some grey hairs, and a Van Dyck beard. He stands five feet ten, very light in build—almost a lathy figure. He doesn't look a soldier. He wears his regimental uniform, but not smartly; his boots could be better polished; his hair could be better combed. His face is burnt almost as black as a native's and, but for his uniform, he might be easily mistaken for a North Indian. Altogether, his appearance in the Governor-General's Darbar has shattered the brandy-and-elevenses atmosphere and the occupants of the room look suspiciously as if they are about to receive a stranger from another land and not one of their own race.*)

ELLIOT:   Mr Henry Lawrence, sir.

(*Pause.*)

HARDINGE:   (*Looking helpless.*) Oh. Well, I'm blessed.

LAWRENCE:   (*Quite at ease.*) Sir?

HARDINGE:   What's the meaning of this, man? Just look at you.

(*Pointing at him.*)

Did you sleep in these clothes?

CURRIE:   (*Mockingly.*) Perhaps Mr Lawrence did not find time to change, sir.

HARDINGE:   If I didn't need you, young man, I would have you shipped back home at once.

LAWRENCE:   Sir . . .

HARDINGE:   Why, this is disgraceful. You look like a bloody native. Your hair needs cutting. Your boots need shining, your shirt needs buttons—

(*Softly.*)

I hope your breeches stay up.

CURRIE:   (*Contemptuously.*) Your Excellency, we should be thankful that Mr Lawrence is at least wearing his regimental colours. Normally, I am told, he finds native dress more comfortable.

HARDINGE:   (*Astonished.*) What? . . . what, what, brandy! Elliot, some brandy . . . *Koi hai?*

(*Elliot replaces Hardinge's tumbler.*)

LAWRENCE:   May I sit down, sir?

HARDINGE:   Certainly. (*Realizing.*)

What, what?

LAWRENCE:   Thank you, sir.

HARDINGE:   Quite, quite.

> (*Pause.*)

Vile stuff

> (*Takes another swig.*)

. . . Elliot bring the Punjab brief.

> (*Elliot does so.*)

Tch, tch.

> (*Muttering.*)

Messy business, the Punjab.

LAWRENCE:   Sir?

HARDINGE:   Lawrence, you've been in the Punjab longer than probably anyone I know. What do you think of the Treaty of Lahore we signed last week?

LAWRENCE:   What treaty?

> (*Quick glances between Hardinge, Currie, and Elliot.*)

HARDINGE:   Come on man, you haven't heard of the Treaty of Lahore? Currie, didn't you send him a copy?

CURRIE:   There was no time, sir. It was signed on Tuesday afternoon and Mr Lawrence had already left by Friday.

HARDINGE:   Read then, Currie. Read.

CURRIE:   What, sir?

HARDINGE:   The document, of course.

CURRIE:   (*Produces a parchment and begins to read.*) 'Whereas on this ninth day of March in the year of our Lord eighteen hundred and forty-six, The Honourable East India Company . . .'

HARDINGE:   Just sum it up. Currie.

CURRIE:   (*Clears throat, slightly flustered.*) Ahem!

> (*Pause.*)

HARDINGE:   Come on.

CURRIE:   By the Treaty of Lahore, the Sikh Kingdom surrenders, in full, sovereignty of the territory, hill and plain, lying between the Sutlej and Beas rivers.

> (*Hardinge beams triumphantly.*)

Two, agrees to pay one and a half crores of rupees indemnity as expenses of the war.

LAWRENCE:   (*Whistles in astonishment.*) Whew! They'll never be able to pay that! Their soldiers haven't been paid for six months.

CURRIE:   Mr Lawrence, you have been asked to listen to the treaty and not comment on the Governor-General's political policy.

(*Bland smile.*)

May I continue?

HARDINGE:   Go on, Currie.

CURRIE:   (*Reading.*) Three, reduction of the Sikh army to 20,000 infantry and 12,000 cavalry; four, surrender of 36 guns apart from those captured in the campaign; five, control of the rivers Beas and Sutlej to the confluence of the Indus at Mithankot.

LAWRENCE:   Unthinkable! They could never keep these terms.

HARDINGE:   Why not?

LAWRENCE:   These're much too harsh.

HARDINGE:   Quite. Now let's not get unpleasant, Lawrence. Quite. Have a drink. Here's to the Punjab!

(*All—except for Lawrence—drink a toast.*)

Splendid.

(*Pause.*)

Tell us, Lawrence, when did the old boy pop off?

LAWRENCE:   'Old boy?'

HARDINGE:   What do they call him? The two-eyed Lion?

LAWRENCE:   The One-eyed Lion. You mean the late Maharaja Ranjit Singh of the Punjab.

HARDINGE:   Quite, quite.

LAWRENCE:   He died in 1839, sir.

HARDINGE:   Quite, that's seven years ago.

LAWRENCE:   (*Smiling.*) Quite.

HARDINGE:   What, what. Quite, quite, quite. What sort of a chap was he?

LAWRENCE:   (*Smiling.*) 'The old boy?'

HARDINGE:   Yes.

LAWRENCE:   He was the greatest ruler Hindustan has known.

CURRIE:   Apart from the British of course.

(*Lawrence smiles back.*)

CURRIE:   (*Contemptuously.*) It would appear that Mr Lawrence's romantic admiration for the late ruler of the Punjab makes him lose perspective.

LAWRENCE:   On the contrary.

CURRIE:   (*Taunting.*) Perhaps he will accord some of that admiration to the military record of the East India Company in India.

LAWRENCE:   I have the highest admiration for the Company's record. There's a difference, however, between greatness and military records.

HARDINGE:   (*Bursting out.*) Touché, what!

CURRIE:   (*Triumphantly.*) Tell us then, Mr Lawrence, why the 'mighty' kingdom of the 'great' Maharaja fell three weeks ago?

HARDINGE:   Yes, yes, Lawrence. That's a bit of puzzle to us. I, for one, never dreamt we'd be in the Punjab so quickly.

LAWRENCE:   I don't think it has fallen.

ELLIOT:   But they've signed the peace treaty.

LAWRENCE:   (*Coldly.*) Treaties are meant to be broken. They are not a beaten people yet.
(*Softly.*)
When their army is betrayed by their own leaders, it is hardly a feather in *our* cap.

CURRIE:   Neither is it a cause for regret.

LAWRENCE:   Nor a cause for joy—for a fairly fought battle would have resulted differently.

HARDINGE:   Elliot, how many men did we lose?

ELLIOT:   Final figures are not yet in, sir.

HARDINGE:   Quite. But why has the Punjab kingdom come to this end?

CURRIE:   Very simple, sir. It's clearly a matter of racial superiority. Every pagan power, no matter how formidable in appearance, must succumb to the civilizing mission of the white races.

HARDINGE:   Lawrence?
(*Pause. Lawrence doesn't seem to have heard. He appears lost in his own thoughts.*)
Come on, man.

LAWRENCE:   (*Realizing.*) Sir?

HARDINGE:   What do you have to say?

LAWRENCE:   (*Matter-of-factly.*) I don't think it's as simple as that. Ranjit Singh died seven years ago. Since his death there's been chaos everywhere and a fierce struggle for succession. The Sardars have been quarrelling like dogs. And understandably, sir. For he not only created the Punjab from a mass of petty states—in fact his personality united the kingdom. He established no institutions which could live after him. When he died, the Punjab died.

CURRIE:   Mr Lawrence seems to have become a true Oriental: he argues through the method of contradiction.

LAWRENCE:  I don't contradict myself. Ranjit Singh is not dead.

CURRIE:    Perhaps he's been on a holiday? (*Bland smile.*)

LAWRENCE:  He still lives in the hearts of the people. It only needs a leader to conjure his memory and rally the people round him. That's why, sir, I think such punitive terms should not be imposed and the dignity of this land should be preserved.

CURRIE:    I find no dignity among people who eat with their hands.

LAWRENCE:  (*Continuing.*) A strongly independent Punjab will be our best buffer against the loose, unruly hordes of Central Asia. Our treaty terms deny the possibility of any stable native government. Who will rule the Darbar under these conditions?

HARDINGE:  (*Smugly.*) The British Government doesn't wish to interfere in the internal affairs of the Lahore Darbar.

LAWRENCE:  But that's exactly what we're doing, sir.

HARDINGE:  Damn it, all right; but we do not intend the Punjab to be an independent state. The young Prince must be under our protection, and do our bidding.

LAWRENCE:  What about his mother, sir?

HARDINGE:  That tart!

LAWRENCE:  I beg your pardon?

HARDINGE:  She . . . she's your headache. Mind you, Lawrence, she's spirited as no other woman I've seen. You'll have to watch her closely. If there's trouble in the Punjab, she's bound to be behind it.

LAWRENCE:  *I* watch her, sir?

HARDINGE:  Yes, Lawrence.

(*Gets up. Lawrence follows; Hardinge looks for the orders and hands them over to Lawrence ceremoniously.*)

In consideration of your generous services in the Punjab, in view of your knowledge of the North-West territories, I, Henry Hardinge, the Right Honourable Governor-General of India and her Majesty's Most Honourable Privy Council hereby appoint you Agent of the Honourable East India Company to the Government of His Highness Dalip Singh, the son of Maharaja Ranjit Singh.

(*Pause. Looks at Lawrence whose head is lowered.*)

Come man, show some sign of life. You're promoted to the Residentship . . . the destiny of the entire North-West is now in your hands.

LAWRENCE:  About the one and a half crores, they can't pay it.

HARDINGE:  Good God! I know they can't.

LAWRENCE:   Then why . . .

HARDINGE:   Because if they're unable to pay, they will have to cede all territory between rivers Beas and Indus including Kashmir and Hazara. (*Almost stealthily.*)

This I figure to be worth about one and a half crores.

LAWRENCE:   Sir, of all the . . .

HARDINGE:   That will be enough, Mr Lawrence. (*Gets up.*)

Good luck in Lahore. Anything you would like?

LAWRENCE:   Yes, sir. I would like to select my own officers.

HARDINGE:   What . . . yes, yes. I think we can arrange that, Elliot. I must run along. Good luck, Lawrence. Conduct yourself like a gentleman and don't kill more natives than you can help. (*Exit.*)

> (*Lights fade, as Hardinge marches out to the sound of the Bengal Infantry March. Remaining characters move away towards stage right. Lights return to suggest a more democratic atmosphere in which Elliot, Currie, and Lawrence are talking. Scene is the same.*)

CURRIE:   (*Derisively.*) What gems of the Indian Empire can we offer the next Ranjit Singh?

> (*Pause. Lawrence doesn't answer. Instead he turns around as if he is looking for someone.*)

Mr Lawrence, I am talking to you.

LAWRENCE:   (*Feigning surprise.*) Oh!

CURRIE:   Who're you looking for?

LAWRENCE:   (*Innocently.*) Ranjit Singh.

CURRIE:   (*Angrily.*) We have a clown to contend with, Elliot, in addition to an Oriental. Mr Lawrence, the days of Clive, Hastings and the Nabobs are gone. This is the age of administering India. India is no more one great adventure. We need regular sorts, not charlatans.

ELLIOT:   (*Appeasingly.*) Ah, ah, what sort of men would you like, Mr Lawrence?

CURRIE:   Probably natives!

LAWRENCE:   As a matter of fact I did have a native officer in mind.

CURRIE:   (*Shocked.*) What?

LAWRENCE:   His name is Sher Singh, the son of Chattar Singh of Attari, who was governor of the North-West Frontier districts under His late Highness. He comes from one of the leading Sikh families. I've known him for five years, and he's a capable young man.

> (*Sher Singh quietly enters and sits down unceremoniously beside Lawrence. He looks on with a matter-of-fact air.*)

CURRIE:     (*As if he has seen a ghost.*) What's *that*?

LAWRENCE:     (*Calmly.*) What's what?

CURRIE:     (*Horrified.*) That!

LAWRENCE:     (*Quietly.*) That is Sher Singh.

CURRIE:     How nice! How nice to meet you Mr Sher Singh . . .

SHER SINGH:     (*Correcting.*) Sardar Sher Singh.

CURRIE:     (*Astonished.*) What?

LAWRENCE:     (*Explaining.*) Not 'Mister' but 'Sardar' Sher Singh.

CURRIE:     How nice, 'Sardar' Sher Singh. Now kindly get out.

LAWRENCE:     (*Firmly.*) He will go out with me.

CURRIE:     Come on, Elliot. I think we're only crowding Mr Lawrence's style.
(*They turn to leave.*)
Ah, I've a young man, Lumsden, who I'd like you to take along.

LAWRENCE:     If you wish.

CURRIE:     I do. (*Turning back again.*)
A word of advice, Mr Lawrence. I hope you will restrain your orientalism and keep the natives at a distance. Keep them in their place if you have to rule them.

LAWRENCE:     Who's going to rule anyone! His Highness Dalip Singh is the Maharaja. His mother is the Regent. Sardar Lal Singh is the Wazir. I am merely the agent of a friendly power.

CURRIE:     Come, come Mr Lawrence.

LAWRENCE:     (*Emphatically.*) As for treating the people, I will simply do for them as I would have them do for me.
(*Exeunt Currie and Elliot.*)

LAWRENCE:     Sher Singh?

SHER SINGH:     (*Elegantly bowing.*) The one and only.

LAWRENCE:     What brings you here?

SHER SINGH:     Breathing the fresh air of the Sutlej.

LAWRENCE:     I mean here?

SHER SINGH:     Just following my nose.

LAWRENCE:     And what does the nose say?

SHER SINGH:     The nose says that my friend Larins is going up in the world. And he needs my help.

LAWRENCE:     (*Raising his eyebrows.*) Oh? How does Sher Singh's nose come to this conclusion?

SHER SINGH:     Because Sher Singh follows the advice of the wise man of our land. Unlike you Angrez who keep your noses up, we keep our noses down.

LAWRENCE:     (*Tongue in cheek.*) Ah, that explains the difference. Obviously we have not been making good use of our noses.

SHER SINGH:     There are noses and noses.

LAWRENCE:     Ah, I see.

SHER SINGH:     Yes.

LAWRENCE:     And with that we end today's dissertation on noses.
(*Seriously.*)
Sher Singh, I'm appointed the Resident at Lahore.

SHER SINGH:     (*Lets out a loud cry, and leaps and embraces Lawrence.*) Wah, wah Larins! It is written. Ever since the day my grandmother read your horoscope, I said to myself, Larins is to become a great man. It is written. You are merely reaping the fruit of your past lives, Larins. I mean Larins *Sahib*. Now you are a big man I must call you 'Sahib'— Resident Sahib.
(*And he bows.*)

LAWRENCE:     (*Trying to cope with Sher Singh's burst of enthusiasm.*) What's written, or where it's written, I don't know. I do know that keeping the Darbar together and honouring the Treaty are not going to be easy.

SHER SINGH:     (*Dismissing Lawrence's difficulties with an easy flourish.*) You leave the Darbar to me. It's easy to handle a Sardar. (*Confidentially.*) You know why? Because he's not very smart. Wah, I'm an old hand at this game. Besides they're my own flesh and blood, aren't they?

LAWRENCE:     Which side are *you* on?

SHER SINGH:     I know you, my friend. And that's enough for me. If you can repeat your triumphs of Ferozepur in the whole of the Punjab, then the Punjab will forget the One-eyed Lion.
(*Pause.*)
Can I join you, Larins?

LAWRENCE:     Don't be a fool, Sher Singh. How will the Sardars take it?

SHER SINGH:     (*Hurt.*) You don't want me?

LAWRENCE:     Of course I want you. You've a brilliant career ahead of you in the Darbar. As the future brother-in-law of His Highness, you're likely to be one of the most powerful men in the Punjab. Why do you want to spoil it?

SHER SINGH:     I don't want brilliance that way. I want to earn it, just like you. Just like the One-eyed Lion.

LAWRENCE:     Are you sure?

SHER SINGH:     Only God can be sure. For myself, I know what I want.

Together we'll do for the Punjab in a year what the Lion couldn't all his life.

LAWRENCE:     (*Admonishing.*) Don't speak like that about His late Highness. He was a great man. We should be lucky if we can continue his work.

SHER SINGH:     (*Jeering.*) Ha, ha, Larins. You're still under his spell. You know what the wise man of our land says:

'Among the blind, the one-eyed is king!'

LAWRENCE:     (*Sharply.*) Is that how the One-eyed Lion was king?

SHER SINGH:     (*Appeasingly.*) No, no.

LAWRENCE:     All right, Sher Singh, come.

SHER SINGH:     (*Giving Lawrence a manly hug.*) Let's go to Lahore.

Lawrence:     Yes, let's go.

# Act One Scene 2

❦

*A month later. Lahore, a town on the banks of the Ravi—capital of the Punjab. The private apartments of H.H. Dalip Singh. It is late evening and the elderly Baba is reading to the twelve-year-old Maharaja.*

BABA:     (*Reading.*) . . . and the crane asked, 'What is the road to heaven?'
DALIP:    (*Interrupting.*) I know. Can I answer?
BABA:     What?
DALIP:    Truthfulness!
BABA:     'And how does a man find happiness?' next asked the crane . . .
DALIP:    By mastering his ego!
BABA.     'When is a man loved?' was the crane's third question.
DALIP:    When he's without vanity!
BABA:     Finally the crane asked, 'of all the world's wonders, which is the most wonderful?'
DALIP:    That no man, though he sees others dying, thinks *he* will ever die!
BABA:     'Right,' said the crane, and with that transformed himself into . . .
DALIP:    (*Bored.*) *Bas,* Baba. Why do we have to read the same old thing every night? Why don't you tell me about the war with the Angrez.
BABA:     No, your Highness. There are dark corners . . . .
DALIP:    Yes, yes. I want to hear about Sobraon and Ferozshahr.
BABA:     Shh, your Highness.
DALIP:    (*Loudly.*) I command you.
BABA:     No.
DALIP:    (*Shouting.*) Yes.
BABA:     (*Reluctantly.*) But don't repeat these words. You know our Khalsa were winning at Sobraon. And we were about to inflict a terrible defeat on the British.
          (*Pause.*)
DALIP:    Go on, Baba.
BABA:     No.
DALIP:    You must tell me.
BABA:     (*Uncomfortably.*) Just as the British were falling back to a second line of defence, they received a secret message from your Commander-in-Chief.

DALIP:   (*Savagely.*) Tej Singh!

BABA:   Shh!

DALIP:   What did the message say?

BABA:   (*Almost whispering.*) That your army's left flank was unguarded. So the Angrez put all his forces there. Your Sardars then called a retreat, leaving the entire Sikh army in confusion. Your Commander-in-Chief fled back across the Sutlej, along with the Wazir, and also broke the bridge over the river. The Sardars, thus, not only betrayed their soldiers but also cut the retreat of the army!

DALIP:   Traitors! The dirty traitors! Lal Singh! Tej Singh! I'll kill them.

BABA:   Shh! your Highness. They will be rewarded according to their karma.

DALIP:   (*Suddenly.*) Go away, Baba. I'll call you when I want to sleep.
(*Baba leaves. Dalip goes towards the balcony. Sound of footsteps, and Rani Jindan enters quickly as a mother enters her child's room. She is about thirty, and definitely attractive.*)

RANI:   Dalip! Dalip! (*She goes over to the bed, expecting to find her son there.*) Why—where—? (*Loudly.*)
My *lal!*
(*Dalip looks into the room; she runs towards him and clasps him.*)
Out in the cold night air? Not in bed yet? Where's Baba?

DALIP:   (*Quite lost, and still looking outside.*) I threw him out. I wanted to be alone.

RANI:   My *lal*, you must sleep now.

DALIP:   Don't *lal* me, Mai. Haven't you already got a *lal*?

RANI:   (*Admonishing.*) Shh . . . (*She slaps him lightly, and he lets out a yell.*) You mustn't talk this way. Who's been teaching you these mischievous things?

DALIP:   Nobody.

RANI:   Why, if I tell this to Raja Sahib, he would be so offended.

DALIP:   Let him be.

RANI:   My child, why are you against him so? He's a nice man. And so important now after the Treaty. He's the Wazir of the Punjab! Until you are old enough, Raja Sahib will rule the kingdom.

DALIP:   (*Mimicking the way of obsequious courtiers.*) It's always Raja Sahib this . . . Raja Sahib that . . .

RANI:   Shh . . . my child.

DALIP:   But I'm the king, Mai. Why is it that no one looks up to me?

(*Proudly.*) During my father's days there used to be such fear of the king. You said so yourself.

(*Pause.*)

RANI:  Dalip, do you know what day it is?

DALIP:  It's my father's birthday. But Mai, why aren't there any lights? There's no music and dancing as we have every year.

RANI:  We've lost a war, child. The state treasury is empty. We owe the Angrez more than one crore rupees.

DALIP:  How much money is that, Mai?

RANI:  It's a lot of money, my son. And the army still has to be paid.

DALIP:  I thought we were the strongest and the richest country in the whole world.

RANI:  We were—in the days of your father.

DALIP:  Why aren't we now?

RANI:  (*Determinedly.*) We will be, my boy. Wait, we will be.

DALIP:  When, Mai?

RANI:  Soon.

DALIP:  When I grow up?

RANI:  Yes.

DALIP:  What will I be like when I grow up?

RANI:  You'll be strong like a lion—just like your father.

DALIP:  (*Enthusiastically.*) Yes, I'll be the Lion of Victory. I'll throw them out. (*Takes out his toy sword from his belt.*)

I'll fight them all and defeat them. Just like my father. I'll win victory after victory. When I have defeated them all, then I'll fight the Angrez. And I'll defeat him too.

(*Wiping her eyes, Rani rushes to him and embraces him.*)

RANI:  Yes, yes. You'll defeat them all. But not tonight. Now it's time for milk and then bed. I'll call Baba.

DALIP:  Do we have to defeat the Angrez?

RANI:  Why?

DALIP:  Because then Larins Sahib will go away. I like him. He taught me to shoot a gun.

RANI:  Has he been talking to you?

DALIP:  Yes, he's my friend. He plays with me.

RANI:  (*More to herself.*) You mustn't see him alone.

DALIP:  Why, Mai?

RANI:  Enough questions now. Off you go. If you want to be brave and strong like your father, go drink your milk and to bed.

DALIP:    Is it true that father drank five seers of milk a day?

RANI:    Oof! More questions.

DALIP:    Then I'll win victories?

RANI:    Yes.

DALIP:    (*Suddenly.*) Mai, I'm afraid.

RANI:    Of what, my boy?

DALIP:    I get bad dreams.

RANI:    A brave boy like you who is going to conquer the whole of Hindustan, you shouldn't be afraid.

DALIP:    But I am.

RANI:    You know what your father used to say about bad dreams. He said the surest way to escape a pursuing tiger is to turn yourself into one. Then he won't touch you. So with everything else. Just become whatever is going to hurt you.

    (*Lal Singh is announced.*)

RANI:    (*In greeting.*) *Sat-Sri-akal*, Raja Sahib. Bow to your elders, my boy.

DALIP:    (*Drawing back.*) No.

LAL SINGH:    What's the matter, your Highness?

    (*Goes towards Dalip, who recoils.*)

    You don't want my blessings?

    (*Softly.*)

    What's the trouble, my lad?

DALIP:    Go away! I don't like you.

RANI:    (*Sharply.*) What! What sort of a behaviour is this? (*She goes over to him, but he runs to the other side.*)

    Come here.

DALIP:    Mai, he's a traitor.

LAL SINGH:    Your Highness, what's this silly talk? You don't believe all this nonsense?

RANI:    Naughty boy. I think it's past his bed-time. I'll call Baba. Let's go away, Raja Sahib. I am sorry for this . . .

DALIP:    Why, Mai? He's a traitor.

LAL SINGH:    Again the same silly thing. What do you mean, child?

DALIP:    What happened at Sobraon, Mai?

LAL SINGH:    (*Firmly.*) What happened at Sobraon, sir?

RANI:    I think this has gone far enough.

LAL SINGH:    No, I want to know. Who's been talking to this boy?

RANI:    Raja Sahib, he's tired. Let's stop this nonsense. We must find who's been filling the boy's ears . . .

LAL SINGH:    The Company Angrez has been spending a lot of time with him.

DALIP:    No. It's not the Resident Sahib.

(*Knocking. Royal ADC enters, and delivers a message to Lal Singh.*)

ADC:    *Hazur!*

LAL SINGH:    Speak of the devil. The Resident Sahib awaits our pleasure on an urgent development in the town.

RANI:    (*To the ADC.*) Send him in.

LAL SINGH:    Here?

RANI:    Why not? (*To the ADC.*)

Go. (*She whispers something in Lal Singh's ear, then goes to the boy who is near the balcony.*)

My boy, your friend, the Resident Sahib, will soon be up here. Ask him to wait. We will be back in a minute.

(*They go and hide behind the curtain. Henry Lawrence enters with the ADC ahead of him. The ADC salutes. Not finding anyone, he salutes again, clicking his heels. Dalip peeps in.*)

DALIP:    (*To the ADC.*) You may go. The others will soon be here.

(*Pause.*)

LAWRENCE:    (*Bows, oriental fashion*) The Governor-General's Agent presents greetings to His Highness.

(*Dalip nods.*)

I came to see your mother and the Wazir, your Highness.

DALIP:    His Highness, the Maharaja of the Punjab, Peshawar, Jammu and Multan presents his salaams to the Resident Sahib. The Rani Sahiba and the Wazir Sahib will be here shortly.

LAWRENCE:    (*Goes to him affectionately.*) So young man, what keeps you up so late? I'm told you're usually in bed by now.

DALIP:    (*Enthusiastically.*) Larins, I shot five perfect ones today.

(*Whispers something in Lawrence's ear. Lawrence moves towards the curtain.*)

LAWRENCE:    Bravo! You're going to be a great shot!

DALIP:    Oh, but not as good as you. You're perfect, Larins. When are we going on *shikar*?

(*Lawrence winks at Dalip. Then points to the right end of the curtain. Dalip shakes his head and points to the left.*)

DALIP:    Larins, do you know the way to heaven?

LAWRENCE:    No. What is it?

DALIP:    I know. Truthfulness.

    (*Lawrence stands motionless before the curtain.*)

LAWRENCE:    Someone is not going to heaven. 'How now? a rat? Dead for a ducat, dead!'

    (*Lifts his foot, and gives a huge kick to the left end of the curtain. The response is immediate.*)

LAL SINGH:    (*A yell of pain.*) Hai!

    (*Comes out from behind the curtain, holding his leg. Rani is also revealed. Exit Dalip.*)

LAWRENCE:    Sorry, Raja Sahib. I had no idea you were back here. I was just trying to kill a . . . a . . . a . . . rat.

RANI:    A rat?

LAWRENCE:    Yes.

RANI:    (*Sarcastically.*) The Angrez has a funny manner of killing rats.

LAWRENCE:    We always kill them this way in England.

RANI:    (*Angrily.*) In future, you might care to leave the palace rats to the palace cats. The Treaty gives the Agent no jurisdiction to act within the palace.

LAWRENCE:    Yes, Rani Sahiba.

RANI:    State your business, please.

LAWRENCE:    (*Bowing in proper fashion.*) The Governor-General's Agent presents salutations to the esteemed Queen Mother and Regent, and his Lordship, the Wazir of the Darbar.

RANI:    (*Coldly.*) The Queen Mother's salaams to the Resident Sahib.

LAL SINGH:    (*Still smarting from the kick on his shin.*) The Wazir's salaams to the Resident Sahib.

LAWRENCE:    Please accept the Governor-General's greetings on this auspicious day.

    (*Hands a document to Lal Singh.*)

RANI:    (*Ironically.*) We are touched by the Angrez Government's gesture.

LAWRENCE:    (*Brushing aside the irony.*) It isn't every day that we share in the glory of the Lion of the Punjab.

    (*To Lal Singh, who appears to be making an effort over the document.*) May I read it, sir?

LAL SINGH:    That won't be necessary.

LAWRENCE:    Perhaps, if your Excellency turned it upside down, it would be easier . . .

RANI:    Your sarcasm is lost, Resident Sahib.

LAWRENCE:   We beg a hundred pardons.

RANI:   Begging comes easy to the Angrez.

LAWRENCE:   Begging is the only course before a beautiful woman.

RANI:   (*Ruffled, but quickly recovering.*) False chivalry doesn't win laurels in our country.

LAWRENCE:   What about true chivalry?

RANI:   Exists only among horses.

LAWRENCE:   The Rani doesn't do justice to men.

RANI:   There are men and *men*.

LAWRENCE:   (*Laughs.*) No. There are men and *women*.

RANI:   (*Frustrated.*) Oh . . . to have such thick-headed Residents is surely the fate of the most unfortunate among God's creatures.

LAWRENCE:   The unfortunate creatures have the sympathy of the Resident.

RANI:   Before the Resident becomes too generous will he be pleased to state his business?

LAWRENCE:   He will be honoured. (*Suddenly in changed tone.*)
   I came to inform you of two things. The Khalsa at Bannu led by the English officers has isolated the difficult tribes, and things are on the way to normalcy on the Frontier.

RANI:   (*Coldly.*) Our congratulations!

LAWRENCE:   (*Exaggeratedly.*) Thank you.

RANI:   What else?

LAWRENCE:   A most unfortunate incident has just occurred near the Shah' alami Gate. Please accept my regrets and those of the entire English establishment at Lahore.

RANI:   (*Urgently.*) What's happened?

LAWRENCE:   (*Uncomfortably.*) A small detachment of English soldiers was crossing the Gate towards the bazaar, when the officer in command found their way blocked by a couple of cows. Not attuned to Indian sympathies, and being young and impetuous, I'm afraid he cleared the street in the quickest possible way.

RANI:   (*Genuinely.*) Hai! He killed the cows.

LAWRENCE:   (*Apologetically.*) I'm afraid so.

RANI:   No!

LAL SINGH:   What sacrilege!

LAWRENCE:   I'm extremely sorry.

LAL SINGH:   He butchered Mother Cow!

LAWRENCE:   It's most unfortunate.

RANI:     Then what happened?

LAWRENCE:     The citizens of the area reacted as expected and our men were barely able to make it alive to the barracks.

(*Pause.*)

If you wish, the young officer and I will make a public apology to the citizens of Lahore tomorrow morning.

RANI:     (*Sharply.*) That's the least you can do.

LAWRENCE:     (*Apologetically.*) If there's anything else we can do, I'd be happy to . . .

LAL SINGH:     The young man will have to come to trial.

LAWRENCE:     (*Firmly.*) I'm afraid that may not be possible. He can only be tried according to the rules of the Honourable Company. However, I intend to deal with him as severely as I can. Please rest assured that this will not happen again.

(*Pause.*)

I have a request.

RANI:     The Angrez has no lack of requests.

LAWRENCE:     (*Unperturbed.*) I request you to arrange for a special guard around the Shah' alami area and the Residency tonight.

RANI:     Anything else?

LAWRENCE:     No, thank you. Good night!

(*Exit.*)

LAL SINGH:     (*Furious.*) The son of a pig! I'm going to burn the Residency tonight.

RANI:     (*Calmly.*) No, my sparrow, I'll handle him.

(*Pause. She smiles.*)

LAL SINGH:     Why do you smile?

RANI:     You know, my sparrow, I like our Resident. (*More to herself.*) Yes, I like him. He has something . . .

LAL SINGH:     (*Muttering.*) That's not surprising.

RANI:     (*Sharply.*) What do you mean?

LAL SINGH:     (*Appeasing.*) You know what I mean.

(*She slaps him.*)

RANI:     If you're jealous, at least be civilized about it. (*Sensuously.*) Our Resident is full of fire.

(*Suddenly.*)

What's your lackey doing in the hall?

LAL SINGH:     Who? Tej Singh?

RANI:       Yes, I can see him at the door. He's trying his best to hear what we are saying.

LAL SINGH:  Rani Sahiba, I beg of you to be more polite to the ministers and the officials of the Darbar. Tej Singh is the Commander-in-Chief of our army, and . . .

RANI:       They're all lackeys! I'm tired. Good night. (*Exit.*)

(*Enter Tej Singh from the opposite side.*)

TEJ SINGH:  (*Laughing.*) Ho, ho, ho!

LAL SINGH:  What are you laughing about, you son of an owl!

TEJ SINGH:  The way she slapped you. Ho, ho, ho!

LAL SINGH:  Shut up, you owl. She called *you* a lackey.

TEJ SINGH:  (*Hurt.*) Did she?

(*Pause.*)

LAL SINGH:  The Angrez Resident is clever—perhaps too clever for his own good. He might upset our plans.

TEJ SINGH:  (*Proudly.*) I can teach him a lesson.

LAL SINGH:  You can't, you peasant. Do you realize who he is? He is the victorious army's Governor. Besides, he can take on ten of your kind.

TEJ SINGH:  (*Hurt.*) Yes?

LAL SINGH:  To make matters worse, someone's been talking to the boy.

TEJ SINGH:  Who?

LAL SINGH:  You village peasant, why don't you think for yourself? Do you think I have all the answers? Sometimes I think your mother forgot to feed you her milk.

TEJ SINGH:  (*Undaunted.*) Is it the Angrez?

LAL SINGH:  No. He's different; he wouldn't do this. (*Suddenly in a whisper.*) Anyhow our work may be easy. The Angrez is going to make a public apology in the Shah' alami Gate tomorrow. Perhaps that is the time to act.

TEJ SINGH:  (*Impressed.*) You are clever, Wazir Sahib.

LAL SINGH:  Shh!

# Act One Scene 3

*The Residency at Lahore, an hour later. Lawrence's young men, including Sher Singh, are lounging about in the Common Room waiting for him. A punkah is swaying lazily overhead.*

LUMSDEN:   Are you going to the nautch tonight, Abbot?

ABBOT:   (*Yawning.*) The nautch girls sing too long. By the time it gets interesting I'm half asleep.

LUMSDEN:   Pretty awful business if you ask me.

ABBOT:   How's your black wench, Lumsden?

LUMSDEN:   Not good.

EDWARDES:   Oh?

LUMSDEN:   She is pregnant.

ABBOT:   So soon.

SHER SINGH:   (*Laughing.*) Ha, ha, That's what happens. First there is woman, then there are children. Ha, ha.

LUMSDEN:   (*Snubbing.*) Shut up, funny man.

SHER SINGH:   (*Quietly.*) I didn't mean any offence.

LUMSDEN:   You can't afford to offend us. Don't forget that you are a native, funny man.

EDWARDES:   Don't, Lumsden.

LUMSDEN:   Natives should speak only when spoken to.

SHER SINGH:   (*Getting up.*) Are you trying to provoke me?

EDWARDES:   (*Appeasing.*) All right, Sher Singh. Enough, Lumsden. No one's going anywhere tonight.
     (*Pause.*)
You've landed us into a fine mess with that silly cow, eh Lumsden.

ABBOT:   I'm not sure if I wouldn't have done the same thing.

EDWARDES:   For God's sake, he could have let the damn cow pass.

LUMSDEN:   It was blocking the road.

ABBOT:   Anyway, why in heaven's name are the niggers so touchy about cows?

LUMSDEN:   I don't know. You should have seen them though. They rose out of the earth and swarmed behind us like bees as we ran here.

ABBOT:   Why didn't you fire on them?

LUMSDEN:   We were running for our lives . . .

EDWARDES:   I don't understand. If the cow was blocking the road you could have pushed it.

SHER SINGH:   (*Bursting out.*) Ha ha ha! I can see him pushing a cow off the road.

LUMSDEN:   Shut up, black man.

EDWARDES:   Don't bully him, Lumsden.

SHER SINGH:   (*Getting up.*) No one's going to bully me. Mr Lumsden obviously doesn't know the wrath of a Sardar.

> (*Sher Singh knocks Lumsden down. There is a scuffle. Edwardes and Abbot try to break it up. Sound of footsteps, and the two hurriedly come apart. Enter Henry Lawrence. All promptly come to attention. Lawrence looks about silently, blank expression on his face. Long pause.*)

LAWRENCE:   (*Quietly.*) What's happening?

SHER SINGH:   (*Cheerfully.*) Oh, we were having a friendly wrestling match.

LAWRENCE:   (*Quietly.*) I don't think it is the place or the time for physical exercise.

> (*Pause.*)

Come here, Mr Lumsden.

> (*Lumsden steps forward. Lawrence looks at him, then slaps him hard on his cheek.*)

You did it deliberately.

LUMSDEN:   No, sir.

LAWRENCE:   Yes, you did. You killed the cow deliberately and perversely.

LUMSDEN:   It was blocking my way.

LAWRENCE:   No, sir.

LUMSDEN:   Yes.

LAWRENCE:   You lied to me. You went out of your way to kill the cow, knowing all the time that the sensitivities of the people there would be outraged by this.

LUMSDEN:   No.

LAWRENCE:   Get out of my sight. I don't like liars. This time it's only a warning. Next time you will be discharged.

LUMSDEN:   (*Rubbing his cheek.*) I shall have to tell Mr Currie about this.

LAWRENCE:   Get out!

LUMSDEN:   (*Leaving.*) Striking an officer is a serious offence, Mr Lawrence. Calcutta is not going to like it.

LAWRENCE:   Get out!

(*Exit Lumsden.*)

Wait!

(*Lumsden re-enters.*)

You had better go to the downstairs room. There's a full guard outside. Don't move out if you value your life.

(*Exit Lumsden.*)

Gentlemen, you serve your country and your conduct must reflect this.

EDWARDES:    If I may be allowed to speak, sir, I think this is a bit harsh on poor Lumsden.

LAWRENCE:    Mr Edwardes, I am less concerned with the integrity of Mr Lumsden than with the fact that there are at least a thousand persons outside who would be glad to have his head. Fortunately Indians are civilized people and don't resort to violence easily. In another land, we would have been burnt alive.

ABBOT:    The natives aren't Christians, sir. Their odious religion has thousands of ugly Gods and rituals. We aren't expected to know them all, are we?

EDWARDES:    Yes sir, we should keep as far away from them as possible.

LAWRENCE:    Enough! I didn't think I'd hear such disgusting nonsense from two of my best men. Have your forgotten perhaps that these people are also human beings?

(*Pause.*)

You were selected from the entire East India Company. Each of you has something which puts him above all others who have come to make their fortunes in India. You are incapable of becoming 'pukka Indians' . . .

SHER SINGH:    Wah, what's a 'pukka Indian?'

LAWRENCE:    A pukka Indian is an Englishman full of curry and bad Hindustani, with a fat liver and no brains, but with a self-sufficient idea that no one can know India, except through a long experience of brandy, gin, gram-fed mutton, and cheroots.

SHER SINGH:    Wah, wah! A real burra Sahib!

LAWRENCE:    The average Englishman thinks that he's doing someone a favour by being in India. But I thought you were here because you liked being here. If I'm mistaken, let me know now. Better still, get out of India by the next boat.

Undeceive yourselves, if you think by remaining in India you will shoulder someone's burden and march into a hero's sunset. Rest assured, Mr Abbot, the Indian doesn't need anyone's shoulder to lean upon. He can do without the Englishman, who as soon as he sets foot in India eternally pines for London fogs and Surrey greens. Your mission to civilize 'the crafty Hindu' will only result in his losing faith in the English. If you have any doubt, go, for God's sake, go to your 'fresh mornings,' 'gorgeous noons,' and 'dewy eves.'

(*Pause.*)

What do you say, Sher Singh?

SHER SINGH:   What can I say, sir? I'm a 'filthy, black nigger.'

LAWRENCE:   Don't be so bloody sensitive!

SHER SINGH:   (*Hurt.*) I'm not.

LAWRENCE:   You Indians are the most touchy people in the world. Sometimes it's so difficult to talk to you. One's always afraid of hurting you. You know Sher Singh, there's a hunting bird who is so sensitive . . . even if you are standing a hundred feet behind it and you move an inch, its neck will cringe. An Indian is like that. One has to be so careful with you.

SHER SINGH:   I'm not like that.

LAWRENCE:   No, you're not. I'm sorry.

(*Pause.*)

I'm tired now.

(*They get up to leave.*)

EDWARDES:   (*Leaving.*) We don't want to leave sir.

(*Lawrence smiles. Then nods. All leave, except Sher Singh and Lawrence.*)

SHER SINGH:   You're tired, Larins. You haven't eaten anything.

LAWRENCE:   I'm not hungry.

(*Shuts his eyes. Long pause.*)

I feel suddenly at ease.

(*Edwardes re-enters and gives a sealed note to Sher Singh.*)

EDWARDES:   Urgent message for Sher Singh.

SHER SINGH:   (*Opening it.*) You've a visitor, Larins Sahib.

EDWARDES:   Visitor? Who's it at this time?

LAWRENCE:   Whoever it is, send him in.

SHER SINGH:   It is not a 'he,' and *it* wants to see you alone.

EDWARDES:   Who is it?

LAWRENCE:   That's all right. Send *it* in.

EDWARDES:   (*Flabbergasted.*) But, sir, you mustn't see just anyone like this.

You must observe proper protocol and security before you see a
stranger.

LAWRENCE:    (*Smiling.*) Strangeress, you mean?

EDWARDES:    (*Confused.*) Why yes, sir. Sir?

LAWRENCE:    My dear Edwardes, the British Empire wasn't built on
'proper security.'
        (*Pause.*)
Send her in.
        (*Smiling.*)
Gentlemen, if you'll now excuse me.
        (*They withdraw. A veiled woman, tall and stately, slowly and gracefully
        walks in. She is dressed in the courtesan's brocaded and ostentatious
        clothes.*)

RANI:    (*Salaaming.*) Zubheda Begum, the singing queen of Benaras offers
her salaams and services to the Resident Sahib.

LAWRENCE:    (*Elaborately returning her salaams.*) We welcome the Begum.
        (*Pause.*)
But we are at a loss to remember if we asked for the charming favours
of the Singing Queen.

RANI:    The widespread fame of the Resident attracts the Queen as the
flickering light from an earthern lamp attracts the moth of the night.

LAWRENCE:    (*Obviously enjoying himself.*) Such flattery would make even
the Gods blush.

RANI:    Truth is not flattery, Resident Sahib.

LAWRENCE:    Then to be alive, certainly is, Begum Sahiba.

RANI:    Not to one who deserves it.

LAWRENCE:    No one can possibly be deserving of so charming a presence.

RANI:    Immortals humble all presences.

LAWRENCE:    Humility humbles even mortals.

RANI:    'Mortals should *not* presume to become immortal,' said the wise
man.

LAWRENCE:    'It is mortals who become immortal,' replied the fool.

RANI:    The Resident Sahib is accomplished.

LAWRENCE:    The Begum Sahiba is generous.

RANI:    Not any more than the Resident Sahib.
        (*Pause.*)
But the brave and mighty Angrez seems to be afraid.

LAWRENCE:    'Fear is only human,' said the jackal.

RANI:    'But the brave are not afraid,' said the lion.

LAWRENCE:    'Even the bravest are afraid of beautiful women,' said the fox.

RANI:    The Angrez gives and takes with the same hand. Come, why is the brave man afraid?

LAWRENCE:    He's afraid that his charming guest may be the Queen of Lahore. He is afraid that the Queen may have got it into her beautiful head that English Residents are expendable. And he's afraid to dirty this clean spot of Punjab earth with good English blood.

RANI:    (*Lifting her veil.*) The Resident is right and wrong. I am Jindan Kaur, the Regent of the Punjab. But I don't think that Residents are expendable. And I haven't come to murder anyone.

LAWRENCE:    (*Getting up.*) The Honourable East India Company's agent is pleased to re-welcome his distinguished guest.

    (*Pause.*)

May one ask why one is being honoured so?

RANI:    Must there be a reason?

LAWRENCE:    No.

RANI:    (*Seductively.*) Then one has come because one fancies it.

    (*Lawrence smiles. Pause.*)

Is the Resident Sahib happy with the police arrangements at the Shah' alami Gate and around the Residency?

LAWRENCE:    Yes, thank you. The efficiency of the Rani Sahiba is admirable.

    (*She smiles.*)

RANI:    Does the Resident insist on making a public apology?

LAWRENCE:    Yes. Why?

RANI:    Because it is not safe.

    (*Pause.*)

Can one also request the Resident to postpone the Council meetings?

LAWRENCE:    Why?

RANI:    For the same reason.

LAWRENCE:    But surely the wise councillors would not . . .

RANI:    (*Interrupting.*) One can't tell. Brahmins like Diwan Dina Nath may be tempted. Brahmins are especially sensitive about the cow.

LAWRENCE:    We are most impressed by the Rani's concern for our safety. May one ask why the Rani . . .

RANI:    (*Disarmed.*) The Resident is pig-headed! Doesn't he understand if a certain person chooses to come at this hour, against all protocol, she may be concerned for someone's safety.

> (*Uncomfortable pause.*)

Things are not well in the Darbar, Larins.

LAWRENCE:  (*Concerned.*) What is it?

RANI:  You know what happened at Sobraon and Ferozshahr.

LAWRENCE:  (*Embarrassed.*) You mean the . . . the treachery of your officers?

RANI:  Yes, the Sardars are not content with betraying the Khalsa. Now they want bigger things.

LAWRENCE:  What?

RANI:  What do you think?

LAWRENCE:  The throne?

> (*Rani nods.*)

RANI:  They are jealous of Dalip and me. Perhaps they find him too independent.

LAWRENCE:  (*Smiling.*) You mean they find you too independent.

RANI:  (*Trying to smile.*) Well, both of us.

LAWRENCE:  And Lal Singh?

RANI:  What about him.

LAWRENCE:  Is he mixed up in this?

> (*No answer.*)

You won't tell me that anyway.

RANI:  (*With dignity.*) No, I won't tell you that.

> (*Pause.*)

I think that was a vulgar remark.

LAWRENCE:  I'm sorry.

> (*Pause.*)

Are the circumstances of the English victory public?

RANI:  I don't think so.

LAWRENCE:  It's important that they remain a secret.

RANI:  That's just it. They want to open up the whole thing.

LAWRENCE:  And crucify themselves in the process.

RANI:  No—discredit Dalip and me.

LAWRENCE:  How?

RANI:  Because all commands were issued under Dalip's and my name. The treacherous message bore my signature.

> (*Embarrassed.*)

Larins, I don't know anything about wars. I used to sign whatever
they wanted me to.

LAWRENCE:   (*Uncomfortably.*) Rani Sahiba, please let's not go into this . . .

RANI:   (*Hurt.*) Do you think I'm a traitor?

LAWRENCE:   Not you.

    (*Pause.*)

I'm just disappointed with my countrymen.

RANI:   We wouldn't have lost in a fair fight, would we?

LAWRENCE:   (*Obviously uncomfortable.*) No.

    (*Long pause.*)

RANI:   You see, Larins. They want to make the betrayal public and pin the
whole thing on me. Once Ranjit Singh's house is discredited they've a
chance at the throne.

    (*Pause.*)

But they're fools. They don't realize that the future of the Punjab is
in British hands?

LAWRENCE:   Not necessarily.

RANI:   You're modest, Larins. You know as well as I, you're not just a
Resident.

LAWRENCE:   There's one thing you forget. It's not an easy thing to destroy
fifty years of great work.

RANI:   People have short memories.

LAWRENCE:   (*Animated.*) Not for one who creates a nation. What are they
compared to the Lion of Punjab? When I was doing revenue work
on the border in '36, I used to hear of him.

    (*Suddenly.*)

Rani Sahiba, tell me, what was he like?

RANI:   (*Suddenly absorbed.*) Oh, he looked mean. He was small, one-eyed,
and worn out by hard living and debauchery.

    (*Giggles.*)

Do you know Larins, he was totally illiterate?

LAWRENCE:   Was he a good man?

RANI:   He was good to me.

    (*Looking at his intense face.*)

Larins, why are you so concerned with my late husband? I don't
understand. You're suddenly so different when you talk of him. I
noticed it before. Why?

LAWRENCE:   (*Embarrassed.*) I don't know.

RANI:   It's very strange.

LAWRENCE:   (*Persisting.*) Was he a good man?

RANI:   No conqueror is a good man.

LAWRENCE:   He forgot his friends quickly, didn't he?

RANI:   Each man has his ways. He used to say 'a dog in sight is better than a brother out of sight.'

LAWRENCE:   In his own way, I suppose, he was even just.

RANI:   Justice is what suits oneself, isn't it?

LAWRENCE:   No, said the judge, justice is forever.

RANI:   Justice is what the people consider just, said the fool.

(*Pause.*)

Do you know the story of the old woman and her daughter-in-law?

LAWRENCE:   No, but I'll tell you a better story—the story of an uncle and his niece. The cruel uncle passed a law that the body of the girl's brother was to be left unburied on the field, because he had conspired against him. She disobeyed the law and secretly buried her brother. She was arrested, and this is what she said in her defence: 'Your laws are unjust. I obey natural law—law ordained by Heaven and known to every man's conscience. Burying one's brother is *natural justice*, which is not of today or yesterday but eternal.'

RANI:   Oh, let's not talk of eternities.

(*Pause.*)

I betrayed my own soldiers! Maybe ruling a kingdom isn't a woman's work.

LAWRENCE:   You're a Queen.

RANI:   What's the use? The back of the Sikh soldier is broken.

LAWRENCE:   (*Genuinely moved.*) You're a great Queen, Rani Sahiba. You'll always be a Queen. Your husband was the Lion of Punjab. He was the Lion of Victory and he left a great unified nation to his people. You must redeem his life. Your people—you must think of them. You're all they have now in this troubled land.

RANI:   (*Gets up.*) You believe all this, Larins. (*As if in a dream, wondering aloud.*) Yes . . . Yes . . . I must. I am a Queen . . . My poor people. My son . . . Dalip . . .

(*Pause.*)

I must go now.

(*She goes up to him.*)

Oh Larins, I am afraid to like you.

LAWRENCE:   Why?

RANI:   For reasons the Resident understands.

LAWRENCE:   And if the reasons were not there.

RANI:   Then I wouldn't be afraid. (*Pause.*)

Oh Larins. (*She takes his hand.*) Larins, take this. (*Hands him a diamond.*) This is a symbol of our friendship and yours for safe-keeping. It belonged to His Highness and I value it greatly. Don't lose it and don't wear it. I must go now.

(*She gets up.*)

LAWRENCE:   (*Enthusiastically.*) Did it really belong to the Lion?

RANI:   Yes.

(*Lawrence displays it on his robe.*)

Don't wear it, please.

LAWRENCE:   Why?

RANI:   Because it's sacred.

LAWRENCE:   (*Hypnotized.*) It's beautiful!

RANI:   Larins, what's the matter? It seems to make you uneasy.

LAWRENCE:   (*Uneasily.*) Oh no, no.

(*Slowly he recovers, beams suddenly and swaggers about displaying the jewel to an imaginary audience.*)

RANI:   (*Puzzled.*) Please, Larins. Don't.

(*Pause.*)

Are you all right?

LAWRENCE:   (*Absorbed.*) Yes.

RANI:   Then put it away.

HENRY:   (*Recovering.*) Yes. Yes, of course.

RANI:   (*Putting on her veil.*) Zubheda Begum salaams the Resident Sahib, and regrets that she could not interest him in her famous song.

(*Lawrence returns the salaams. Lights fade.*)

# Act Two Scene I

*The Residency. Next day. It is late morning. The air quivers with heat and is full of the scent of white and yellow jasmine. Dust rises and whirls languorously at the slightest breeze. From near at hand comes the long, slow creaking of a Persian wheel, turning lazily. Water comes up and splashes out. Lawrence, Sher Singh, and Edwardes sit talking outside on the verandah. Lawrence is dressed in a chogah and is seated on a charpoy, leaning on a cushion. He smokes a hookah which is occasionally passed around to the other two, who are seated on the same charpoy to his left.*

LAWRENCE: *(Contemplative.)* See those fierce plains, Edwardes! Everything has passed on them.

EDWARDES: Sir?

LAWRENCE: *(Preoccupied.)* Yes, they've all gone by; gone by this field on their way in or out of Hindustan—emperors, generals, saints, and beautiful women. Cities rose here in splendour, cities of the Aryas, the Mauryas . . .

EDWARDES: Cities of the Guptas, Moghuls.

LAWRENCE: They all rose and were destroyed and now lie forgotten among these wheatfields. So many great men passed on this ground—Alexander, Kanishka.

EDWARDES: Harsha, Timur, Babur.

SHER SINGH: What's this—a roll-call?

LAWRENCE: *(Continuing.)* They're only names. The peasant has seen it all. Today, tomorrow, yesterday—it's the peasant who holds the Punjab.

SHER SINGH: Larins Sahib's a philosopher this morning.

EDWARDES: Such glorious dust inspires philosophy even among Company men. Have a drink, sir? Sher Singh?

LAWRENCE: No thanks.

SHER SINGH: I'll have some English wine. You Angrez know how to live.

LAWRENCE: *(Continuing as if no interruption had taken place.)* We are to all appearances more powerful in India than we ever were. Nevertheless, when our downfall comes it will be rapid and the world will wonder more at the suddenness of the Empire's end than at all it achieved.

Empires grow old and perish. Ours in India can hardly be called old, but seems destined to be short-lived—what with that bungling lot in Calcutta. We appear to have passed the brilliance and vigour of our youth, and it may be that we've reached a premature old age. Who knows, Sher Singh, who knows how many will come after the British?

EDWARDES:     But the peasant will always be there.

LAWRENCE:     Yes, the Punjab peasant will always be there. Isn't it reasonable then, that we win him to our side? To win him, we must work for him, for his sake. The memory of the British should rest in the peasant's heart, in his timelessness.

SHER SINGH:     As Sadi says, 'The smoke of the poor man's heart goes up to heaven.'

LAWRENCE:     He also says, 'What matters is to die on a silken pillow, or on the cold earth?'

SHER SINGH:     (Clapping.) Wah, wah! Only a silk pillow's softer.

LAWRENCE:     But death's the same.

SHER SINGH:     A conqueror's talk of the peasant smacks of hypocrisy.

LAWRENCE:     Perhaps.

SHER SINGH:     To the peasant they're all the same.

LAWRENCE:     What do you mean?

SHER SINGH:     The peasant is an excuse for other ambitions.

LAWRENCE:     There's much good we can do for him, Sher Singh.

SHER SINGH:     Ah Larins, even the wisest men forget where good ends and power begins.

LAWRENCE:     (Remembering.) Is it time for the Shah' alami Gate?

EDWARDES:     Yes, sir. I'll go and gather the men.

          (Exit.)

SHER SINGH:     (Noticing a jewel in Lawrence's hand.) Larins, what's that?

LAWRENCE:     (Embarrassed.) Why, a jewel.

SHER SINGH:     Where did you get it?

LAWRENCE:     Do you like it?

SHER SINGH:     Let me see it.

LAWRENCE:     (Embarrassed.) No.

SHER SINGH:     Wah Guru! That's the Koh-i-noor? Who gave it to you? Larins, please return it. You can't wear it.

LAWRENCE:     Why not?

SHER SINGH:     Only His late Highness could wear it.

LAWRENCE:     Why can't I?

SHER SINGH:    (*Panicky.*) Larins, put it away. You'll spoil everything. The
people won't like it. Give it back.

LAWRENCE:    No.

   (*Embarrassed pause as Lawrence's face shows him struggling with
   himself. Suddenly replaces it in his pocket.*)

SHER SINGH:    Let's go, Larins Sahib!

   (*Exeunt.*)

# Act Two Scene 2

꧁꧂

*Shah' alami Gate, Lahore. Half an hour later. Sher Singh, Edwardes, Abbot, and Lumsden are facing the audience and Lawrence is making a speech. Noise of crowd.*

LAWRENCE:    Again, most honoured citizens of Lahore: yesterday's killing of a cow on this spot has grieved me personally. On behalf of the entire English community, I assure you that this will not happen again. Please accept our sincere apologies.

(*Shouts and booing from the crowd.*)

My dear friend, Sher Singh, who, as you know, comes from one of the noblest families . . .

(*Shouts: 'Sher Singh, Angrezi todi.'*)

To convince you of our sincerity, I have decided to waive one month's land revenue for the citizens of this district.

(*Shouts: 'Larins Sahib zindabad.'*)

We want to begin by listening to you, honoured citizens, rather than by ordering you about like 'Lord Sahibs.' We want to build canals, bridges, roads. We want to ensure as much justice as possible to each citizen. We want to prevent the soldiers from interfering in your everyday affairs.

(*Shouts of approval from the crowd: 'Larins Sahib zindabad'; 'Angrez Badshah zindabad.' Suddenly the sounds of musket shots. Confusion.*)

EDWARDES:    I think it's coming from that side.

SHER SINGH:    Larins Sahib, are you hurt?

LAWRENCE:    Just a little. We'd better go.

ABBOT:    My God! And quickly. That one just nicked my hand.

LAWRENCE:    Is anyone hurt? Are you hurt, Abbot?

EDWARDES:    I beg you to get away from the spot, sir.

(*More shots, confused sounds.*)

ABBOT:    I was against coming here at all.

LUMSDEN:    It's obviously a conspiracy. Let's give them an English volley.

LAWRENCE:    No.

LUMSDEN:    (*Muttering.*) I'd like to butcher the whole lot of them.

ABBOT:    Let's teach the niggers a lesson.

LUMSDEN:    Burn the damn street! That's what they deserve . . .

ABBOT:    Filthy heathens!

EDWARDES:    The cheek! We came to apologize, and they take advantage of us.

ABBOT:    This is what we get for treating the natives differently. We've made asses of ourselves.

SHER SINGH:    Shut up, all of you. Larins Sahib is hurt.

(*To Edwardes.*) Help me with his arm. Take him to the Residency. All of you go quickly. I'll stay and try to find out who's behind this.

(*Exeunt all Englishmen. Tej Singh and Lal Singh enter from the shadows.*)

TEJ SINGH:    (*Hidden by shadow of wall.*) Psst Attari! Psst Attari!

(*Sher Singh turns round, his hand on his sword.*)

LAL SINGH:    (*Coming out.*) Sat-sri-akal, Sardar Sahib.

SHER SINGH:    Sat-sri-akal. What are you doing here, Raja Sahib?

LAL SINGH:    (*Ironically.*) An honour to meet you, Sardar Sahib. Since you became such an important man, little people like us rarely have the pleasure.

SHER SINGH:    It isn't every day that we meet a traitor turned Wazir.

LAL SINGH:    On the contrary, it is a rare sight to see a full fledged stooge of the English.

SHER SINGH:    An honest man's a humbler being than a Wazir who betrays his army and his people.

TEJ SINGH:    (*Roaring.*) *Oi! Angrezi chamcha*, be polite to the Wazir.

SHER SINGH:    Speak, what do you want? I'm in a hurry.

TEJ SINGH:    The boy's in a hurry. We fought beside your uncle, Sham Singh. Learn to respect your elders.

SHER SINGH:    (*Aroused.*) Sham Singh was the only hero among cowards and traitors. Don't take his name—you'll only defile it.

TEJ SINGH:    I'll break your head in two, you . . .

LAL SINGH:    (*To Tej Singh.*) Shut up, you son of a pig.

(*Appeasingly to Sher Singh.*)

Now, now, Sardar Sahib, tell us what's it like being with the Angrez?

(*Confidentially.*)

Is it true, they don't bathe?

SHER SINGH:    Is this what you wanted to discuss?

LAL SINGH:    No, Sher.

(*Going up to him and putting his arm around him patronizingly.*)

Now Sher, we've come to you with a proposal. Do you want to remain a slave of the Angrez, or would you like to work for the glory of the Khalsa and the greatness of your land?

SHER SINGH:    With traitors?

LAL SINGH:     Come now, Sher. Let's forget the past, and . . .

SHER SINGH:     (*Interrupting.*) Speak, what do you really want from me?

LAL SINGH:     My friend, we want the Koh-i-noor, which the Rani has given to the Resident.

SHER SINGH:     What makes you think the Resident has got it?

LAL SINGH:     I know everything.

SHER SINGH:     Why do you want it?

TEJ SINGH:     (*Naïvely.*) So we can sell it to Dost Mohamad.

LAL SINGH:     Shut up, you son of an owl. Let me do the talking.

(*To Sher Singh.*) No, my dear friend. It's for the good of the land. I need the diamond to show the Darbar what kind of Queen they have—she's selling our country to the Angrez swine.

SHER SINGH:     A traitor is hardly in a position to judge others.

(*Pause.*)

You dogs, don't you think I know our Rani? Whatever the world may say, whatever her weaknesses, she's the only Rani we have, and her son the only Maharaja. And the Punjab hasn't a better friend than she. Besides, we need her son to keep the kingdom together. So traitors, it's no use trying . . .

LAL SINGH:     (*Interrupting.*) It may be worth your while.

SHER SINGH:     It can't be worth my while.

LAL SINGH:     Even if you could be the next Wazir.

TEJ SINGH:     (*Naïvely.*) I thought I was going to be the Wazir.

LAL SINGH:     Shut up, you village idiot.

SHER SINGH:     Even if you offered me the throne, no.

TEJ SINGH:     The throne is reserved for the Raja Sahib.

LAL SINGH:     Shut up!

SHER SINGH:     Good day, traitors.

LAL SINGH:     Wait! (*Softly.*)

You know I command an ear in Calcutta.

SHER SINGH:     With your Curries and Shurries who made you the Wazir.

LAL SINGH:     It may be prudent for the Resident to turn over the jewel.

SHER SINGH:     Now it's blackmail.

LAL SINGH:     Well, ah, I don't think Calcutta will look too kindly on a Resident accepting such expensive gifts.

SHER SINGH:     If you want to blackmail him, speak to the Resident yourself. Traitors, I have work to do!

# Act two Scene 3

*The Residency, an hour later. Lawrence is sitting on a divan, smoking a hookah. His left arm is heavily bandaged. Enter Rani and Dalip.*

RANI:    (*Admonishingly.*) What has the Resident done to himself? Didn't I warn him not to be a hero?

LAWRENCE:    (*Smiling.*) 'Heroes are foolhardy,' said the lion.

RANI:    'Fools are also foolhardy,' replied the crow.

LAWRENCE:    'Fools have a heart,' said the lion.

RANI:    'The wise have a head,' said the crow.

DALIP:    (*Impatiently.*) Larins, why didn't you shoot them? With your aim, you would have got them easily.

LAWRENCE:    No, my boy. I didn't know who was shooting.
     (*Pause.*)
     Rani Sahiba, where were you and His Highness when this happened?

RANI:    Why, in the palace, of course. You don't think that *we* were shooting, do you?

LAWRENCE:    No. Remember, you told me about the Sardars . . .

RANI:    (*Interrupting.*) Child, why don't you go out and play with Baba?

DALIP:    But I want to be with Larins.

RANI:    Later. Now go.
     (*Exit Dalip.*)
     What about the Sardars?

LAWRENCE:    Nothing specific, Rani Sahiba. I've a feeling that the firing this morning was connected with your conspiracy of the Sardars.

RANI:    You mean, to divert attention.

LAWRENCE:    Somehow I feel their target was in the palace.

RANI:    (*Afraid.*) No! Dalip? No, it couldn't be.

LAWRENCE:    Perhaps not. There's no point speculating.

RANI:    It could well be some lunatic Brahmins who did the firing.

LAWRENCE:    Perhaps.

RANI:    (*Suddenly examining his* chogah.) Larins, what is this? This is my husband's *chogah*. What are you doing with it?

LAWRENCE:    (*Quietly.*) You won't understand, Rani Sahiba.

RANI:      (*Disturbed.*) What are you doing with my husband's robes? Can't you leave him alone? You're obsessed with him.

LAWRENCE:    (*Defensively.*) This has nothing to do with your husband.

RANI      Then what's it all about?

         (*Pause.*)

Tell me—I have a right to know.

LAWRENCE:    A right?

RANI      He was my husband; I am the Regent. Besides, you are my friend, and I want to know what happens to my friend.

LAWRENCE:    One shouldn't know everything about one's friends.

RANI:      I must know.

LAWRENCE:    (*In agony.*) There's nothing to know.

RANI:      (*Sincerely.*) Yes, there is.

LAWRENCE:    You won't understand.

RANI:      I understand too well.

         (*Pause.*)

LAWRENCE:    No.

RANI:      (*Disappointed.*) You're just like the rest of them. I thought there was something different in you, Larins. You were simple, austere, single-minded. Now you're behaving the way the other Ferangis did when they got power under my husband. They became swollen.

         (*Lawrence makes no answer, attempting to hide the traces of an inner conflict. Rani comes closer.*)

Larins, are you all right?

         (*Pause.*)

You were so free of vanity. That's what I liked about you. You were different.

LAWRENCE:    You don't like me now.

RANI:      Of course, I do, silly. I . . . I do. I do. I do, too much. (*Embarrassed.*) Now see what you've made me say.

LAWRENCE:    (*Quietly.*) This is all to be a better Resident, I think. If you Indians respect authority from its appearances, then it's sensible to appear properly, isn't it?

RANI:      I'm only sad that my old Larins is changing. I liked you as you were—a soldier with a purpose.

LAWRENCE:    The purpose isn't lost.

RANI:      I'm afraid it will be, once you start wearing all these things.

LAWRENCE:    For God's sake, what do clothes have to do with it?

RANI:   Nothing. Then why are *you* changing your clothes?

LAWRENCE:   Only to be more effective.

RANI:   Larins, you can do all the things you want—give Darbars in the countryside, mete justice to the people like a king. But don't do it in Lahore. The Sardars will resent it. I don't like it. In Lahore we must keep up appearances. The Resident in Lahore is an Agent of a friendly power to the South. No more.

   (*Pause.*)

Larins, forget about the Lion. There's so much you have done in the Punjab. And there's so much you have to do before Dalip grows up.

LAWRENCE:   But what about this land, will it wait for him to grow up?

RANI:   Together we will make something of the Punjab. You as my Resident, and I as the Rani. We'll make it strong and prosperous—just as in the days of the Lion.

LAWRENCE:   (*Excited.*) Yes, yes, just as it was in the days of the Lion. We'll make it rich and happy. We'll build, build. Build roads, canals, and the land will sing with joy.

RANI:   Oh Larins, I know you will do it too.

LAWRENCE:   (*Glowing.*) Yes, they'll say that the Lion has returned! The Lion has returned!

   (*Pause. Rani watches Lawrence's glowing face.*)

RANI:   (*Tenderly.*) Oh Larins . . . Larins . . .

   (*Lawrence kisses her passionately.*)

Where did you learn that, Larins?

LAWRENCE:   I'm a soldier, remember?

RANI:   (*Sensually.*) Again.

   (*Lawrence suddenly embarrassed. Moves back a little.*)

LAWRENCE:   No.

RANI:   Why?

LAWRENCE:   (*Cold.*) I don't know. I'm sorry.

RANI:   (*Smiling.*) I order you.

LAWRENCE:   No.

RANI:   Oh Larins!

   (*Lights fade.*)

# Act Two Scene 4

*The same. Late afternoon. Two sentries enter.*

FIRST SENTRY:   Has the fire in Shah' alami Gate been put out?

SECOND SENTRY:   They're still fighting it. They've found twenty-four bodies so far. God knows how many more are trapped inside.

FIRST SENTRY:   It's the biggest fire I've seen.

SECOND SENTRY:   They say that the same Angrez captain who killed the cow started the fire.

FIRST SENTRY:   With the Angrez, it looks like bad times are coming.

SECOND SENTRY:   (*Spitting out betel.*) What nonsense you talk! The Angrez has brought peace to our land. My brother says the Khalsa has never got its salary packet so regularly. The peasants worship him.

FIRST SENTRY:   (*Whispering.*) Is it true that the Resident Sahib has been recalled to Calcutta?

SECOND SENTRY:   (*Confidentially.*) The Wazir's a powerful man.

FIRST SENTRY:   And a jealous one.

SECOND SENTRY:   Shh, someone's coming.

(*Enter Lawrence and Lumsden. The two sentries salaam and exit.*)

LAWRENCE:   I think I'm losing my temper.

(*Pause.*)

Do I understand that you burnt a whole street because you thought someone needed to be punished for firing on us. Is that right?

LUMSDEN:   The filthy natives needed to be taught a lesson.

LAWRENCE:   Didn't you know that an investigation to find the culprits behind the firing was under way . . .

LUMSDEN:   (*Savagely*) Investigation by that native, Sher Singh!

LAWRENCE:   Before I lose my temper, it may be prudent for you to leave. I warned you once. You will return at once to Calcutta.

LUMSDEN:   Mr Currie is not going to like this . . .

LAWRENCE:   He is also not going to like your murdering twenty-four people.

LUMSDEN:   (*Shrugging his shoulders.*) Twenty-four natives! I'd burn a thousand filthy natives! Mr Lawrence, I'll tell you something: the entire English community here and in Calcutta will be on my side when the time comes.

LAWRENCE:     (*Losing his temper.*) Get out! Get out, you insubordinate swine, before I kick you out!

LUMSDEN:     Do I get a police escort?

LAWRENCE:     (*Shouting*) Get out!

(*Exit Lumsden.*)

Ho Sipahi!

FIRST SENTRY:     (*Entering.*) *Hazur!*

LAWRENCE:     Send Sher Singh.

(*Exit sentry. Lawrence takes the jewel from his pocket and looks at it admiringly. His anger slowly vanishes and gives way to another emotion. As Sher Singh enters, Lawrence quickly hides it.*)

LAWRENCE:     (*Authoritatively.*) Sher Singh, we need a velvet covering for this divan. Purple colour. (*Goes near the divan and points to the covering.*) This one looks like a rag.

(*Proudly.*)

This is the Residency. We must be dignified. We are going to hold Darbar today.

SHER SINGH:     Darbar?

LAWRENCE:     (*A bit uncomfortable.*) Yes, you know, the Council meeting.

SHER SINGH:     But we've been having Council meetings here in the past. We haven't needed coverings before?

LAWRENCE:     We're going to have them from now. It will be fitting!

SHER SINGH:     (*Dubiously.*) I suppose so.

LAWRENCE:     And some velvet cushions too. Same colour. Both the covering and the cushions must have gold work. That will improve the effect, won't it?

SHER SINGH:     (*Dubiously.*) I suppose so.

LAWRENCE:     And have my initials, H.L., put in gold on them.

SHER SINGH:     (*With a mock flourish, bowing exaggeratedly.*) Yes, Your Most Eminent Highness.

LAWRENCE:     We'll also need a mattress to put on the floor for the Sardars.

SHER SINGH:     (*Pointing to the divan.*) They won't sit here as usual?

LAWRENCE:     No, I think they should sit below.

SHER SINGH:     (*Seriously.*) The Sardars won't like it, sir.

LAWRENCE:     They'll have to.

SHER SINGH:     They only recognize His Highness Dalip Singh, sir.

LAWRENCE:     (*Softly.*) I'm not asking them to recognize me as their ruler.

SHER SINGH:     (*Uncomfortably.*) What does this Darbar mean then?

LAWRENCE:   You don't understand, Sher Singh. (*Moving around the room, thinking aloud.*)

... Now, let's see. The divan should go over there. Perhaps a bit more to the right. That's the way to rule India ... with dignity. I must also get the Residency's exterior lifted a bit. Yes, Indians like colour, pageant, style. They respect it. That's authority for them. This place looks like a barrack—no wonder they think us odd. They like to be ruled through the heart; we rule through the head. They like to be dealt with at the personal level; our basis of administration is impersonal law. They respect tact; our laws and settlements are crudely blunt. You can't change a people's view of the world just like that: Particularly if they've just lost a war ... You've got to be careful. You've got to make them forget they've lost a war ...

(*Long, dreamy pause. Sher Singh looks on uncomfortably.*)

SHER SINGH:   Larins, why have you had the Wazir arrested?

LAWRENCE:   Because he was behind the firing at the Shah' alami Gate.

SHER SINGH:   Larins, you're asking for trouble. Have him released at once. He's a powerful man. He can make life difficult for you.

LAWRENCE:   Sher Singh, are you afraid?

SHER SINGH:   No.

LAWRENCE:   Wasn't he behind the incident?

SHER SINGH:   Yes, he was. The firing was just to divert attention from the attempted kidnapping at the Palace. At the last minute, they lost track of Dalip.

LAWRENCE:   How?

SHER SINGH:   No one knows. When they found they'd failed they laid a bait for me. They offered to make me the Wazir if I'd hand over the Koh-i-noor.

LAWRENCE:   How did they know?

SHER SINGH:   The know.

LAWRENCE:   (*Smiling.*) Don't you want to be the Wazir?

SHER SINGH:   What?

LAWRENCE:   It's a tempting thought.

SHER SINGH:   I respect friendship more.

(*Pause.*)

Larins, please return the jewel to the Rani.

LAWRENCE:   Why?

SHER SINGH:   Because it will only bring trouble.

LAWRENCE: Are you afraid of trouble?

SHER SINGH: No. But I don't seek it.

LAWRENCE: (*Laughs.*) Come on, let's go. The people must be waiting. It's time for Court.

    (*Lights fade. Lawrence and Sher Singh move across to stage right.*)

# Act Two Scene 5

As lights come on, Lawrence is found seated cross-legged on a divan. Sher Singh
is at his side. The people are at a respectful distance. The ragged gathering includes
peasants, beggars, crying children, brahmins, shopkeepers, etc. The assembly has
the look of a Diwan-e-Am, the People's Darbar, and Lawrence appears to be quite
pleased with himself as he sits enjoying the role of a king dispensing justice.
Sher Singh and his incongruously rich robes add to the baroque effect.

OLD WOMAN:    (Pleading.) Hazur Sahib! Larins Sahib! I have a sick child in
    my arms. Can you help me? You will live a thousand years. Please
    help him!

FIRST BRAHMIN:    Don't push. I want to see what's happening.

SECOND BRAHMIN:    I'm not pushing.

OLD WOMAN:    (Wailing.) Larins Sahib, help my sick child. May you walk
    on lakhs . . .

SHER SINGH:    (Abruptly.) Bibi, this is a court of Law, not a hospital. Next
    case!

OLD WOMAN:    (Pleading.) But what can I do, sir? My child—it will die.

SHER SINGH:    (Annoyed.) Bibi, what can we do? Next case!

LAWRENCE:    (Producing a small purse.) Her child's sick, is it?

SHER SINGH:    Yes.

LAWRENCE:    Give her this and tell her to go to the doctor for medicine.
    (Sher Singh does so. Speaks softly to her. She leaves, bowing low and
    shouting: 'May you live a thousand years, Larins Sahib.')

SHER SINGH:    Next case! Are all you sons of swine asleep? Come on. Next
    case!
    (The Prosecutor motions two saffron-robed brahmins to come forward.
    Then he digs into the crowd and comes out leading a lean, fair, young
    girl in a white sari. Her face is partially hidden by the end of her sari,
    which covers her head as well. Sher Singh nudges Lawrence.)
    That's it! Let's have more of this.
    (Lawrence looks reproachfully at Sher Singh.)
    Begin the case, fool! Do you think we're waiting for your grandson
    to be conceived?

PROSECUTOR:    (Authoritatively.) These brahmins, Your Excellency, (the *brahmins bow*) complain that this woman did not commit *sati*, according to tradition, when her husband died last month.

SHER SINGH:    What punishment do you demand?

PROSECUTOR:    Your Excellency, she should be burned alive, according to the custom.

SHER SINGH:    Well, Larins Sahib, I think that's fair.

LAWRENCE:    What's fair?

SHER SINGH:    That she should be burned.

LAWRENCE:    Why?

SHER SINGH:    Because it's the custom.

LAWRENCE:    What does she have to say?

SHER SINGH:    What do you have to say, Bibi?

(*No answer. He speaks more gruffly.*)

Speak, woman. What do you say, commands the Angrez Badshah.

(*No answer. He speaks to the Prosecutor.*)

*Oi*, you ask her.

LAWRENCE:    (*To Sher Singh.*) Why did you call me the Angrez Badshah?

SHER SINGH:    That's a way of speaking. After all they're peasants . . .

LAWRENCE:    But I'm not a king.

SHER SINGH:    (*Defensive.*) Should I address you differently?

LAWRENCE:    (*Embarrassed.*) No, no. I like it. Say it again.

SHER SINGH:    (*Puzzled.*) Angrez Badshah!

LAWRENCE:    No, I mean the whole thing.

SHER SINGH:    What?

LAWRENCE:    What you just said. Something about 'commands the . . .'

SHER SINGH:    (*Puzzled.*) 'What do you say, commands the Angrez Badshah.'

LAWRENCE:    Yes. Now say it with style.

SHER SINGH:    (*Concerned.*) Larins Sahib, are you all right?

LAWRENCE:    (*Embarrassed.*) Yes.

SHER SINGH:    (*Still concerned.*) Maybe it's the heat. Let's go in.

LAWRENCE:    No. Go on.

SHER SINGH:    (*To the Court.*) Next case.

PROSECUTOR:    But, Your Excellency, we have not finished with the present case.

SHER SINGH:    (*More confused.*) All right, same case, then. You sons of swine, do you think we have the whole day?

PROSECUTOR:    She doesn't speak, Your Excellency. She hasn't spoken since her husband died.

SHER SINGH:  How can we deliver justice to . . .

LAWRENCE:  (*Correcting him.*) Natural justice.

SHER SINGH:  (*Puzzled.*) How can we deliver natural justice to the defendant, fool, if she can't speak?

PROSECUTOR:  (*Apologetically.*) Your Excellency, what can we do?

LAWRENCE:  No wonder she doesn't speak. What do you expect her to say when the whole village is ready to burn her. What do the brahmins have to say?

FIRST BRAHMIN:  Maharaj, it's the custom of our land that a holy-wedded wife perform *sati* on the pyre of her Lord and Master, her holy-wedded husband.

SECOND BRAHMIN:  Yes, Your Highness. It's the custom. And this irreligious, immoral woman refuses to abide by the custom by which her ancestors have conducted themselves.

LAWRENCE:  My nation also has a custom. When men burn women alive, we hang them. Let us each act according to our national customs.

FIRST BRAHMIN:  This is not justice. A man has a perfect right to do whatever he wants with his wife. She is his property. If he is angry with her, he can throw her in the well.

   (*Laughs. Others join in.*)

LAWRENCE:  Well, I'm angry. Why shouldn't I throw you in the well? (*Shouts.*)

*Ho Sipahi*, throw these two brahmins into the well.

   (*Sepoy comes forward and leads them away.*)

Sher Singh, we are issuing a proclamation: *sati* is with immediate effect abolished in all provinces and districts of the Punjab. And the Hindu Reform Bill is with immediate effect extended to all parts of the Punjab. Next case!

   (*Applause from the crowd. Shouts of* 'Larins Sahib zindabad.')

SHER SINGH:  Next case, fools.

PROSECUTOR:  Time for recess, sir.

LAWRENCE:  Call the Wazir and the Commander of the Khalsa.

SHER SINGH:  The Wazir?

PROSECUTOR:  The Wazir?

CROWD:  The Wazir?

   (*Confused sounds.*)

SHER SINGH:  You can't call the Wazir here, Larins.

LAWRENCE:  Why not?

SHER SINGH:    (*Uncomfortable.*) You can't. He's too big a man.

LAWRENCE:    Call the Wazir!

SHER SINGH:    Larins, don't. It's bad enough to have arrested him. Don't disgrace him. You're asking for trouble. Besides the Wazir only answers to the Regent. Please don't. Let's go in. The sun's too hot.

LAWRENCE:    Call the Wazir.

(*Lal Singh and Tej Singh are brought in. The latter spits in contempt.*)
Sher Singh, what are the charges?

SHER SINGH:    (*Automatically.*) What are the charges, owl?

PROSECUTOR:    What are the charges, sir?

LAWRENCE:    All right. I shall speak the charges. One, you are charged with an attempt to abduct His Highness Maharaja Dalip Singh and subvert his Raj.

(*Pandemonium among the crowd. Cries, confusion.*)
Two, you are charged with the creation of a conspiracy which resulted in the firing at Shah' alami Gate on the English officers.

(*Confusion again.*)
Three, you are charged with exploiting the war against the English, specifically, the Sobraon battle, to subvert the Raj.

(*More confusion.*)
Speak! What do you have to say in your defence?

(*They spit simultaneously.*)
Is that all you have to say? All right, when you're in a better mood to talk, then we'll talk. *Ho, Sipahi!* Put them in lock-up.

(*Sepoy conducts them out. Crowd applauds loudly. Approving shouts, whistles. 'Larins Sahib zindabad,' 'Angrez Badshah zindabad,' 'Resident Sahib zindabad.'*)

LAWRENCE:    (*To Sher Singh.*) Why are they shouting?

SHER SINGH:    (*Smiling.*) They're happy!

LAWRENCE:    What are they saying?

SHER SINGH:    'Long live Larins Sahib!'

LAWRENCE:—What else?

SHER SINGH:    'Long live the Angrez Badshah!'

LAWRENCE:    (*Glowing.*) Yes, yes, the Angrez Badshah. I'm a hero, Sher Singh.

SHER SINGH:    You're a hero, Larins Sahib!

(*Lights slowly fade. Spot on Lawrence's glowing face. Sound becomes louder. Drums. Triumphant music. Shouting becomes softer, ceases. Music and drums continue.*)

# Act Three Scene I

The Governor-General's headquarters at Fort William, Calcutta—seat of the Government of India. Two weeks later. A map room. Hardinge, Currie, and Elliot are standing before a huge map of North-West India, absorbed in the excitement of Empire-building.

ELLIOT: (Pointing.) What about a penetration from the East?
(Winking.)
I'm sure the Nawab should be agreeable.

CURRIE: Militarily, out of the question. Our hill strategy must be Punjab-based. We must secure the Punjab before we can think of the hills. This is precisely what Lord Ellenborough wrote to Queen Victoria and the Duke of Wellington a few months before he left India.

HARDINGE: (Sarcastically.) Oh, did he?

CURRIE: Yes.

HARDINGE: And would it be expecting too much, Currie, to have you make a point, without naming all the important people you know?

ELLIOT: The hill people are good fighters. It may not be possible, sir, to follow . . .

CURRIE: Of course it's possible. Didn't Sir Charles Napier do it in Sind in '43? And the Baluchis were no mean fighters.

HARDINGE: Napier. Good God man, can't you tell it straight. Napier—can't stand the man myself.

CURRIE: Yes, sir. The Commander-in-Chief thought that the surprise-attack policy of Napier's would be best suited to the hills. Without even Headquarters knowing Napier had Sind.

ELLIOT: It was a magnificent victory, sir.

CURRIE: (Excited.) He surprised the Baluchis at Khairpur with such artistry. And a handful of English soldiers—that's all he had when he marched to Imamgarh. A splendid fight.

ELLIOT: (Excited.) You know the despatch that he sent to your predecessor, sir?

HARDINGE: (Caught in the excitement.) Yes, yes. What was it now?

ELLIOT: 'Peccavi!'

HARDINGE: Peck what?

CURRIE:     Latin, sir. 'I have sinned.'

HARDINGE:     Ho, Ho. 'I have Sind.' That's good. 'I have sinned.' It's funny. Ho, ho! (*Others join in laughter.*)

Ho, ho.

*(Lawrence has quietly entered from stage right. He is wearing his white chogah. He listens to the three Empire-builders, absorbed with Napier's victories in the Sind.)*

LAWRENCE:     (*Quietly.*) That was a sin!

*(All three simultaneously turn around, taken by surprise.)*

HARDINGE:     (*Recovering.*) What the devil! Who are you?

ELLIOT:     (*Recognizing.*) It's Mr Lawrence, I think.

LAWRENCE:     I believe you asked for me, sir.

HARDINGE:     Good God man, what are you up to? Where did you get these silly robes? Still haven't learnt to be a soldier, have you?

CURRIE:     Still cheeky, Mr Lawrence?

*(Hardinge turns round to face the map again. The other two follow suit. Lawrence is left staring at their backs.)*

HARDINGE:     What about the Sind strategy for the hills? (*Pointing to Kashmir on the map.*)

Kashmir! I want Kashmir—lovely place, I hear.

ELLIOT:     That would be difficult, sir. What with Gulab Singh having just paid a million sterling for the *gaddi*, as agreed during the Lahore treaty negotiations . . .

HARDINGE:     We should be able to manage some sort of arrangement with him.

ELLIOT:     It's a delicate matter.

HARDINGE:     I know it's a delicate matter. India's a delicate matter. Don't forget gentlemen, we're the greatest power on this earth today. Everything we do is a delicate matter.

CURRIE:     For the hills, we can adopt the same diplomatic initiative that Napier did in the Sind.

LAWRENCE:     (*Interrupting.*) Napier is a bounder!

*(All three turn round in amazement.)*

HARDINGE:     What, what, what!

LAWRENCE:     Napier is a bounder!

HARDINGE:     Quite, quite. Can't stand the man myself.

LAWRENCE:     The annexation of Sind is a scandal unequalled in modern history.

CURRIE:    Mr Lawrence, your advice will be sought when necessary. Kindly wait outside till we are done.

LAWRENCE:    I have been asked *in* here by the Governor-General.

HARDINGE:    (*Feeling uncomfortable.*) Quite, quite. This bloody heat!

ELLIOT:    That's India, sir. Will you have a drink?

HARDINGE:    Yes, yes, Elliot. A drink, good idea.

(*Elliot fetches it from stage left.*)

Now what were you saying, Currie?

CURRIE:    I can't say very much, sir, while that man stands there . . .

HARDINGE:    Come on, Lawrence. We're discussing something important. Yes, Currie.

(*They turn to face the map again.*)

CURRIE:    I was saying in summary that our policy towards the hills should be as bold as Napier's was in Sind. As soon as the Punjab is annexed we should plan a Punjab-based campaign in the hills. If all goes well, by January next year you should be able to present Her Majesty with the Western Himalayas.

LAWRENCE:    Acquired through deceit and treachery.

(*They turn round again.*)

HARDINGE:    Quite. Come on, Lawrence. Quit making a nuisance of yourself. (*Moves to stage left and sits down on a chair. The other two follow suit. Lawrence remains standing at stage right. The room assumes a strange, sinister appearance—a mock court, as it were.*)

Why has Lawrence been called back to Calcutta?

CURRIE:    The list of charges is rather long, sir.

LAWRENCE:    Charges?

CURRIE:    (*Smiling.*) Charges.

HARDINGE:    What are the charges?

CURRIE:    (*Reading.*) First, the unauthorized and unnecessary arrest of our most faithful allies and friends in the Punjab kingdom—the Wazir, Lal Singh, and the Army Commander, Tej Singh.

HARDINGE:    (*Shaking his head.*) Serious matter!

CURRIE:    Two, the unsanctioned release of one month's revenue of Lahore district, and abdicating his revenue responsibilities for the entire Punjab.

HARDINGE:    Next.

CURRIE:    Three, behaving in a manner not becoming the dignity of the Governor-General's Agent in the incident known as the 'cow row.'

HARDINGE:    Hmpf!

CURRIE:    Four, pre-emptory dismissal of one of the best officers of the company.

HARDINGE:    Next.

CURRIE:    Five, employing and favouring a native officer.

HARDINGE:    Anything else?

CURRIE:    Six, accepting valuable gifts without informing his superiors.

HARDINGE:    Is that all?

CURRIE:    Yes sir.

(*Pause. The three look at each other in a meaningful way.*)

HARDINGE:    (*Generously.*) Do you have anything to say for yourself, Lawrence?

LAWRENCE:    Have I been called fifteen hundred miles to answer these ridiculous questions?

CURRIE:    You're speaking to the Governor-General, sir.

LAWRENCE:    Yes, sir.

HARDINGE:    (*Impatiently.*) What do you have to say, sir?

LAWRENCE:    Nothing, sir.

ALL THREE:    (*Astonished.*) Nothing?

LAWRENCE:    Nothing, sir.

(*Uneasy pause.*)

HARDINGE:    Come on man, you must have something to say.

(*Silence.*)

CURRIE:    (*Triumphantly.*) Well, if he has nothing to say, then he's obviously guilty.

LAWRENCE:    (*Calmly.*) May I be excused, sir?

(*Long, uneasy pause. Hardinge, perplexed at the unexpected outcome, finally gets up and goes to Lawrence.*)

HARDINGE:    (*Appeasing.*) Come on Lawrence, you must have some answer to these charges.

LAWRENCE:    (*Correcting him.*) These *questions*. (*Coolly.*)

The traitors Lal Singh and Tej Singh are subverting the Raj of His Highness, and they deserve . . .

CURRIE:    They're our friends.

LAWRENCE:    They're traitors.

HARDINGE:    They may be useful to us one day. Release them. Apologize to the Wazir and make the other one a Raja on the day of honours. This is politics, Lawrence. Next?

CURRIE:  The revenue problem, sir.

HARDINGE:  Lawrence, we've been concerned by the lack of revenue the Punjab is yielding.

CURRIE:  (*Correcting.*) By the lack of revenue Mr Lawrence is *collecting*, sir.

LAWRENCE:  We're still making a just settlement. It will take us a few more months before we can start the collection process.

HARDINGE:  In the meantime, the Punjab is costing us money, young man. You must get on with it. I have to answer to impatient Directors.

LAWRENCE:  But our revenue settlement should be *just*, shouldn't it?

HARDINGE:  I'm afraid the Directors are far more concerned with the balance sheet than justice.

LAWRENCE:  In the long run, I believe, it is our just dealings with the people that will make us respected.

CURRIE:  It isn't respect that we desire, Mr Lawrence. It is revenue and the natives will have to accept that.

LAWRENCE:  In the end, a contented people will give far greater returns. History shows that arbitrary governments never last for very long.

CURRIE:  In the end, our interest is to annex the Punjab.

LAWRENCE:  They've just begun to have confidence in themselves, and now we want to take away their honour. It's hardly fair, is it?

HARDINGE:  Mr Lawrence, political affairs are not conducted on fairness. Self-interest is the only motive.

LAWRENCE:  Annexing the Punjab at this time will not be in our interest either.

HARDINGE:  Why not?

LAWRENCE:  Because the Punjab borders Afghanistan and is too close to Russia. I don't think we want to take on either. Least of all do I think we're prepared for the uncivilized hordes of Central Asia. If we leave the Punjab alone, it is their problem. Thus, the Punjab serves as our cushion in India. And at the same time, we honour our promises and treaties with their leaders.

HARDINGE:  There's something in what you say. But 'leaders'—that's precisely the problem. There are no leaders. With that woman there, nothing can be certain. And it will not change either. She's schooling the boy in intrigue, and he will grow up to be no different.

CURRIE:  There's no doubt, sir. She's a terrible influence on the boy. We must separate her from him.

LAWRENCE:  Separate a mother from her son?

CURRIE:    Yes.

LAWRENCE:    One doesn't do these things in India.

CURRIE:    I've heard she's again involved in some intrigue against the other nobles. Things are much too unstable with her there. She will have to go, I'm afraid.

LAWRENCE:    But she's the Regent.

CURRIE:    That can be managed. Lal Singh can be a good Regent.

LAWRENCE:    The boy detests him.

CURRIE:    The boy can always be schooled.

LAWRENCE:    How will you convince the people? She's the wife of the late Maharaja, who was a God to his people. She's the only symbol, besides her son, of legitimate authority.

HARDINGE:    You will have to find some excuse for the people, I suppose.

LAWRENCE:    That will not be possible, sir. We will undo all that we have achieved at a stroke.

CURRIE:    (*Maliciously.*) Perhaps Mr Lawrence's persistence is a reflection of his personal relations with the Queen. And we shouldn't press too far, sir.

HARDINGE:    What?

CURRIE:    Oh nothing, nothing really. Just that I had heard certain things which might, you know . . .

LAWRENCE:    (*Sharply.*) What have you heard?

CURRIE:    Really one needn't go into it here. It's rather a delicate. . . .

LAWRENCE:    (*Firmly.*) I want to go into it here.

HARDINGE:    Come on, Lawrence. It's not necessary to go into details.

LAWRENCE:    Yes, it is.

CURRIE:    It would be in bad taste to discuss it here.

LAWRENCE:    You'd be advised to.

HARDINGE:    (*Appeasingly.*) Come on, Lawrence. I'm sure Currie didn't mean any harm.

(*Lawrence moves towards Currie.*)

CURRIE:    (*Visibly afraid.*) Sir, the man really means it.

LAWRENCE:    (*Shouting.*) Answer, Mr Currie.

CURRIE:    (*Petrified.*) Oh, nothing really. I've heard . . . I've heard that your relations with that woman are, you know, you know . . .

LAWRENCE:    I don't know.

CURRIE:    (*Meekly.*) You know, rather advanced.

LAWRENCE:    Who told you?

CURRIE:   I won't say.

LAWRENCE:   You won't?

   (*And he advances on Currie, who tries to dodge him.*)

CURRIE:   (*Pleading.*) Sir, the man's mad. Elliot, call someone.

LAWRENCE:   (*Coolly.*) Rest assured Mr Currie, I'm not mad. But for your sake, you'd better answer.

CURRIE:   (*Reluctantly.*) It was Lal Singh.

HARDINGE:   Who?

LAWRENCE:   The Wazir. He's Mr Currie's spy, and a former lover of the Queen Mother.

HARDINGE:   So he's jealous of her. Now Lawrence, there's no need to go any further. Currie, I want a complete report on your associations with this man. I need hardly say, Currie, that this reflects rather badly on you.

ELLIOT:   In fairness to Mr Lawrence, sir, Mr Currie should withdraw his remark.

CURRIE:   (*Still scared.*) I withdraw my remark.

HARDINGE:   Was there anything more we needed to discuss with Lawrence?

CURRIE:   (*Very softly.*) Yes sir.

HARDINGE:   Speak up, man.

CURRIE:   (*Softly.*) Yes sir.

HARDINGE:   Speak up. Have you lost your voice?

CURRIE:   If we could discuss it another time, sir.

HARDINGE:   Let's hear it now.

CURRIE:   The jewel, sir.

HARDINGE:   Yes, yes, Lawrence. I want that jewel. I'm afraid the Directors have promised it to Her Majesty. It's to form a part of the Crown jewels in London.

LAWRENCE:   That won't be possible, sir. The jewel isn't mine. It belongs to the Rani and the Maharaja's family. It was only loaned to me as a symbol of her faith in us.

HARDINGE:   I'm afraid I must have it.

LAWRENCE:   I'm sorry, sir.

HARDINGE:   Well, well. We can talk about it later.

   (*Pause.*)

What's next, Currie?

CURRIE:   Nothing, sir.

HARDINGE:   Elliot?

ELLIOT:   Nothing more, sir. Except, I feel, we owe Mr Lawrence our congratulations. In no part of India is there so much popular sentiment in our favour. It's all due to him. He's a hero there, sir.

(*Goes up to Lawrence and shakes his hand.*)

Congratulations, Mr Lawrence. I'm going back home on furlough, and I'll tell the family that I had the honour of shaking hands with you.

HARDINGE:   What about you, Currie?

CURRIE:   No thanks, sir.

HARDINGE:   Come on, Lawrence. Have dinner with me. (*They turn to leave.*)

Tell me more about this jewel. What do they call it?

LAWRENCE:   (*With a swagger.*) The Koh-i-noor, sir.

(*Exit Hardinge with Lawrence.*)

# Act Three Scene 2

𒀸

*Lahore. A week later. Lawrence sits troubled in one corner of the Diwan-e-Khas. It is early, and the courtiers have not yet arrived for the Royal Darbar. He is wearing Ranjit Singh's jewel and chogah. Other parts of the Lion's dress, including a turban, are nearby. The mental transference is nearly complete.*

HARDINGE'S VOICE:  (*Off.*) I know it's a delicate matter. India's a delicate matter. Don't forget gentlemen, we're the greatest power on this earth today. Everything we do is a delicate matter.

LAWRENCE:  (*Angrily.*) No!

(*Long pause. Anger on Lawrence's face turns to pain. He gets up, paces the room then sits down and covers his face with his hands, letting out a soft moan. Continues to brood. Quickly gets up again, and paces the room more furiously. He goes to the window on the left. Resists a temptation to break it. Returns.*)

Oh no! Damn it, no!

CURRIE'S VOICE:  (*Off.*) There's no doubt, sir. She's a terrible influence on the boy. We must separate her . . .

(*Pause.*)

Things are much too unstable with her there. She will have to go, I'm afraid.

LAWRENCE:  (*In agony.*) Oh God! What are they doing? What are they doing to me?

(*Suddenly gets up in anger. Goes to window, and breaks it. Blood begins to run from his hand. He tries to wipe it off with the chogah, but only stains the robe. Enter Sher Singh. Lawrence quickly hides his bleeding hand.*)

SHER SINGH:  What is the Resident Sahib doing in here so early? Everyone is looking for him.

(*Suddenly sees his hand.*)

Larins, you're bleeding! What have you done to yourself?

LAWRENCE:  (*Shouting.*) Leave me alone!

SHER SINGH:  (*Trying to help him with his hand.*) Tch, tch, Larins, you shouldn't go about spilling good English blood.

LAWRENCE:  Leave me alone.

SHER SINGH:    (*Humouring him.*) Come on, Larins . . .

LAWRENCE:    (*Interrupting.*) And call me the 'Angrez Badshah'!

SHER SINGH:    (*Humouring him.*) All right, 'Angrez Badshah.' Now come on, Larins, we have to dress your hand before the Darbar.

LAWRENCE:    (*Shouting.*) Call me the Angrez Badshah!

SHER SINGH:    *Wah Guru!* You really mean that! Look at your eyes.

(*Lawrence goes to the side and inspects his eyes in a mirror.*)

LAWRENCE:    (*Coolly.*) Of course I mean it.

(*Pause.*)

Now dress me!

SHER SINGH:    (*Shocked.*) What!

LAWRENCE:    (*Calmly.*) Help me with those things.

SHER SINGH:    The Maharaja's . . .

LAWRENCE:    (*Interrupting.*) Yes.

SHER SINGH:    No!

LAWRENCE:    Yes.

SHER SINGH:    (*Panicky.*) Larins, what's the matter?

LAWRENCE:    (*Shouting.*) Call me the Angrez Badshah!

SHER SINGH:    (*Sadly.*) Let's go back to the Residency.

LAWRENCE:    (*Calmly.*) If you won't dress me, I shall do so myself.

(*Begins to dress himself in the Lion's ornaments slowly and deliberately. Finally he puts the turban on his head, very carefully. Sher Singh looks on, disappointed and helpless. Lawrence goes in front of the mirror, looks admiringly at himself, and shouts 'Angrez Badshah.' White spotlight on his glowing face as other lights fade.*)

LAWRENCE:    Angrez Badshah! Angrez Badshah!

(*Puts his hand with the diamond condescendingly before him.*)

Bow down to the Angrez Badshah! Bow down, you Lal Singhs and Tej Singhs. You can kiss the jewel. The Punjab is mine, as surely as the Koh-i-noor is mine.

Where is my Rani? In the harem, is she? So much the better.

Where is my son? Asleep. Let him sleep. He needs his sleep.

The tribes are restless? We shall teach the tribes. They are dealing with a great Badshah of a great land. Let's go on to battle. The Lion has come.

(*He yells.*) Arhh!

(*Light fades.*)

# Act Three Scene 3

🥀

*The same. A few minutes later. Full lights on Diwan-e-Khas. A chaotic, noisy, but splendid assembly of Hindu, Sikh and Muslim nobles. His Highness Dalip Singh sits in the centre on a throne. Rani and Lal Singh sit on the divan nearby. Others are on the floor. Lawrence standing between the throne and the divan, is finishing his speech to the Court.*

LAWRENCE: And finally I want to thank His Highness and the noble Darbar for listening to me so patiently. Please be assured that the British Government will try to act to the mutual advantage of both the Punjab and the Company. Our policy on land revenue is one example. Our policy on the Frontier is another. My apologies to the Wazir Sahib again. It was truly an unfortunate incident—a misunderstanding, which resulted in a hasty arrest.

COURTIER: Don't let it be repeated.

SECOND COURTIER: What about the Wazir's plot against His Highness?

CROWD: Yes, yes. What about the plot against the government?

LAWRENCE: The Wazir has already rendered apologies to the government for his indiscretions.

SECOND COURTIER: Has the government accepted?

LAL SINGH: (*Getting up.*) Of course they have accepted.

CROWD: No, no. We want the Wazir to apologize.

LAL SINGH: Shut up, you pigs.

CROWD: No, no.

LAWRENCE: I think you'd better apologize, Lal Singh.

LAL SINGH: (*Condescendingly.*) I apologize.

LAWRENCE: Is the Darbar satisfied?

CROWD: Yes, yes. The Wazir is right. The Angrez is right. Resident Sahib zindabad! Wazir Sahib zindabad!

LAWRENCE: Thank you. Now I beg permission of His Highness, the Rani Sahiba, the Wazir Sahib and the illustrious Darbar's indulgence to proceed with the ceremony of the day of honours. The Governor-General has been kind enough to recommend honours to fifteen nobles of the Punjab.

HERALD: (*Announcing in a magnificent voice.*) The concluding and most honoured event of the Darbar will now take place in the auspicious presence of and with the cosmic blessing of the all-powerful, all-knowing, all-conquering His Highness, the Maharaja, by the Guru's grace firmly established in his kingdom and bringing prosperity and strength to the Khalsaji—His Highness!

CROWD:    May he live long! May His Highness live long!

HERALD:    To fulfil the special request of our honoured and bountiful ally to our South, the Honourable East India Company and the Right Honourable the Governor-General of India, and one of Her Majesty's Most Honourable Privy Council . . .

CROWD:    May he live long!

HERALD:    His Highness, as a special favour to our esteemed ally who is represented by the most honoured ambassador, Mistar Hendri Larins . . .

CROWD:    Larins Sahib zindabad! Larins Sahib!

HERALD:    His Highness will confer titles and honours on fifteen nobles of our court.

(*Shouts, clapping, music, noise.*)

The first and foremost Sardar of our court, the brave and noble Sardar Tej Singh, the Commander-in-Chief of the Khalsa, is to receive the first honour; from today he will be addressed as Raja Tej Singh.

CROWD:    Raja Tej Singh, may he live long! Raja Tej Singh!

HERALD:    The magnificent Raja will now step forth to be blessed by His Highness with the sacred tikka, as a mark of his new status . . . Raja Sahib!

(*Tej Singh steps forward and kneels before Dalip. Lawrence personally takes the golden plate containing saffron to Dalip, who instead of placing the tikka on Tej Singh's forehead, shrinks back into his seat. Immediate commotion among the crowd. Confusion and noise.*)

LAWRENCE:    Your Highness!

TEJ SINGH:    Your Highness!

CROWD:    Your Highness!

(*Dalip snatches the plate from Lawrence, and turns it upside down over the head of Tej Singh. With his left foot, Dalip kicks the Sardar, who loses his balance and falls down. Laughter among the crowd. Noise, shouts. Lawrence, red with anger, looks at the Rani, who turns away.*)

CROWD:    May His Highness live long!

(*More commotion. Noise.*)

LAWRENCE: (*Clapping his hands for attention.*) His Highness regrets his inability to continue with the rest of the proceedings. The Darbar is dismissed.

DALIP: (*To Lawrence.*) I hate you, Larins. I hate you!

(*Dalip runs away with Lawrence staring after him.*)

CROWD:—May His Highness live long!

(*Crowd begins to disperse quickly. Lawrence looks around for the Rani, who has already left.*)

LAWRENCE: (*To Tej Singh, sprawled on the floor*). Off with you. Get out before you have to lick any more boots, you dog. The Darbar is over.

(*Exit Tej Singh.*)

LAWRENCE: (*To Sher Singh.*) Inform the palace that I wish to wait on the Rani Sahiba urgently.

SHER SINGH: Yes, Larins Sahib.

(*Exit.*)

(*The last of the magnificent Darbaris leaves. Lawrence, alone in the Diwan-e-Khas, slowly moves across towards the mirror, adjusting his robes as he does so. After a long and admiring look at himself in the mirror, he slowly, deliberately moves towards the throne. Checking an initial impulse to sit on it, he walks behind it instead. He appears to be undecided, looks about him, and finally sits on the left arm of the throne. Long pause as he stares into space. Re-enter Sher Singh.*)

SHER SINGH: I've informed the palace, sir, that you seek an audience with the Rani Sahiba.

LAWRENCE: (*Absentmindedly.*) Thank you.

SHER SINGH: (*Still smarting from the insult.*) The cheek of that boy! Why do you think he did it?

LAWRENCE: (*Quite lost.*) Eh?

SHER SINGH: (*Continuing.*) Not only does he insult the Commander-in-Chief—not only does he refuse to put the tikka on his forehead, but he also kicks poor Tej Sigh.

LAWRENCE: (*Ironically.*) Poor Tej Singh?

SHER SINGH: Well, the poor man didn't quite expect this on his day of glory.

LAWRENCE: He should have.

SHER SINGH: This is hardly something his greatest admirer should say.

LAWRENCE: Who?

SHER SINGH: You put him at the head of the list of honours.

LAWRENCE:   There are reasons of policy.

SHER SINGH:   There are also reasons of honour.

LAWRENCE:   An Englishman learns to master his feelings.

(*Pause.*)

SHER SINGH:   I wonder how the boy got it into his head?

(*Pause.*)

I suppose His Highness really must detest Tej Singh. He must have done this . . .

LAWRENCE:   No, someone else is behind it.

SHER SINGH:   His Highness knows Tej Singh is a traitor. Ever since Ferozshahr and Sobraon . . .

LAWRENCE:   (*Impatiently.*) I know, I know. But the boy's not capable of doing this on his own.

SHER SINGH:   Then it must be Lal Singh.

LAWRENCE:   It can't be the Wazir, because the boy hates his guts. It can only be the Rani.

(*Rani suddenly bursts in, obviously agitated.*)

RANI:   Larins, Larins!

(*Lawrence nods to Sher Singh, who goes out quickly.*)

Since when have you needed to wait on me?

LAWRENCE:   (*Embarrassed.*) Well, ah . . .

RANI:   Don't be a coward. Say it.

LAWRENCE:   Why?

RANI:   Why? I should ask 'why.' That son of a pig deserved it. You want to know if I put Dalip up to it. Yes, I did. And I'm not at all sorry for what my son did.

(*Pause.*)

LAWRENCE:   Why, why did you have to meddle with this?

RANI:   You Angrez have been helping that traitor from the beginning. Now you've made him a Raja. It's disgusting! Half the Punjab knows he's a scoundrel and just because he does your dirty work . . .

LAWRENCE:   Tej Singh's a useful man.

RANI:   . . . and apologizing to Lal Singh like that. I've never been so humiliated.

LAWRENCE:   Matters of policy, I'm afraid.

RANI:   (*Suddenly breaks down.*) Oh Larins! Larins, why are we talking like fools: *You* and *me; yours* and *mine.* It's *ours*, isn't it? You've always . . . no, we've always wanted what was best for the Punjab. Larins, why did you do it?

LAWRENCE:  Why did *you* do it?

RANI:  I don't know . . . because I hate him.

LAWRENCE:  It was wrong.

RANI:  Why did you put that scoundrel's name at the head of the list? I thought you didn't like him either, Larins.

LAWRENCE:  I don't. But you've insulted my Government.

RANI:  But you, Larins, you're more important.

LAWRENCE:  No, not always.

RANI:  (*Puzzled.*) Something's wrong. Why has my Lawrence changed so much? Next he will want to put his own name on the list. (*Goes to him.*) Oh Larins, then it's true?

LAWRENCE:  What?

RANI:  Larins, I'm afraid. I'm afraid something terrible's going to happen soon.

  (*No response. Lawrence stares away blankly.*)

LAWRENCE:  I'm afraid you'll have to leave.

RANI:  All right Larins, I'll go back to the palace. When you feel better, come to see me. I shall be waiting.

LAWRENCE:  I mean you'll have to go far away . . . far away from here—Sheikhupura.

RANI:  (*Turning pale.*) Why?

LAWRENCE:  (*Smiling.*) Because my Government wants it.

RANI:  You're joking?

LAWRENCE:  No.

RANI:  Why?

LAWRENCE:  Because those are my orders.

RANI:  You're my friend, Larins; how can you ask me to go away?

LAWRENCE:  Yes, I'm your friend. That's precisely why you must go.

RANI:  But I'm the Queen. I'm the Regent. My son's the King of the Punjab. How can I go? Of course you're joking.

LAWRENCE:  No, you're no longer the Regent.

RANI:  Since when?

LAWRENCE:  Since now.

RANI:  And my son?

LAWRENCE:  He remains where he is.

RANI:  The King?

LAWRENCE:  Yes.

RANI:  You're taking my son away from me?

LAWRENCE:  He's the King.

RANI:  He's my son.

> (*Lawrence makes no reply. Rani almost hysterical.*)

He's my son, and no one's going to take my son away from me.

> (*Lawrence still makes no reply. Rani continues to look expectantly at his expressionless face.*)

Oh God, what have I done? Why are they doing this to me? (*Suddenly calm.*)

Yes, I know. I know they're angry in heaven. I betrayed the Punjab, and it's their payment for Sobraon. It's their retribution. Larins, do you really think I deserve this? Tell me, do I?

> (*Pause. Silence. Lawrence staring like a statue. Rani animated.*)

I've got you. I have-got-you. Why only me? Why do you pick on me? The pigs Lal Singh, Tej Singh—They were all responsible. They're equally guilty. And Tej Singh, the biggest scoundrel, you've made him a Raja. Is this your English justice? Tej Singh, the Commander-in-Chief, who cut his own army's retreat. What could be a bigger crime? Why blame only me? I didn't even fight.

(*Quiet again. Silence, goes closer to Lawrence and takes his hand.*) Larins, say something. Why don't you say something? I don't mind . . . tell me that I'm wrong. I'm strong. But say something.

> (*Suddenly concerned.*)

Are you all right? Then, why don't you speak?

> (*She slaps him lightly on the face. He reacts. She smiles.*)

Larins, I don't want to leave you.

> (*Puts her head on his chest.*)

I want to love you. Why are you sending me away? Don't you love me any more? Tell me you don't love me. For God's sake, say something.

> (*Quiet again. Lawrence is like a stone. Rani continues to lean on his shoulder. Long pause. Suddenly she draws away.*)

You can't do this to me! Angrez or the Angrez's father can't touch me. Does the Angrez realize who I am?

> (*Slowly, deliberately imperiously.*)

I am the Mother of the Punjab. I am the wife of the One-eyed Lion. You won't dare! I am the Mother of the Khalsa. Touch me and you'll

have mutiny on your hands. Once I leave, a curse falls on the Angrez.
And the first one to go will be you, Larins.

    (*Pause.*)

Give me back my jewel!

LAWRENCE:   (*Hiding the jewel behind his back.*) No.

RANI:   It's mine. Give it back.

LAWRENCE:   No.

    (*She tries to grab it unsuccessfully.*)

RANI:   Why?

LAWRENCE:   I can't. The Governor-General has promised it to Queen
Victoria.

RANI:   Oh Larins! I gave it to you as a symbol of my faith—a symbol of
our friendship. No!

    (*Pause.*)

Is this how you treat a Queen? You are dirty like the rest of the Ferangis.
Never learn manners. There are ways of treating kings and queens.
Do you know what the defeated Porus, king of the Punjab, answered
Alexander? Alexander asked him, 'Porus, how shall I treat you now?'
Porus replied, 'Treat me as a king treats a king.' And Alexander did so.

    (*Pause.*)

You're intoxicated, Larins! Something demonic is urging you on to
your destruction. Believe me.

    (*Pause.*)

God, now I understand your robes, your Darbars, and your 'Angrez
Badshahs.' It all fits. And your obsession with my late husband. You're
drunk, my friend. Power's gone to your head. And you've forgotten
your friends.

LAWRENCE:   That's not true!

RANI:   Of course it's true. My old Larins is no more.

LAWRENCE:   No.

RANI:   It is and you know it. (*Pause. Softly.*)

When are you sending me away?

LAWRENCE:   Today.

RANI:   No! I'll run away. I'll hide. (*Pause. Pleading.*)

Will no one come and help? Will no one say 'Stay, Rani, stay.' You
Sardars—I don't expect anything from you. I'd love to kill you, you
sons of pigs. You're happy, I know, to get me out of the way. I spit on
you—all of you. You fools, you don't realize that the same fate awaits

you. Your game is over. The Punjab belongs to the Angrez. The One-eyed Lion is dead today! (*Hysterical.*)

The Khalsa! Yes, the Khalsa will save me.

(*Pause.*)

Isn't there a Sikh who needs me? What's happened to you, men? I, the Mother of the Khalsa; I, the holy-wedded wife of the Lion; I need you. Where's your heart, men? Has the Angrez reduced you to fighting for money? Where's your honour? Shame!

(*Pause.*)

Dalip! Dalip! Where are you, Dalip? Have you too forgotten me? Dalip!

(*Offstage sound of Dalip's voice shouting faintly.* 'Mai, mai.')

There he is! (*Begins to cry. Dalip enters.*)

DALIP:   Mai, I was looking for you. (*Rushes into her open arms.*)

Mai, do you know . . . (*Interrupts himself.*)

Mai, you're crying!

(*Pointing to Lawrence.*)

Is Larins making you cry?

RANI:   No, my boy.

DALIP:   (*To Lawrence.*) Larins Sahib, I don't like you any more. Why do make my mother cry?

(*Rushes towards Lawrence as if to kick him, but Rani pulls him back before he can touch Lawrence.*)

*You* dismissed my Darbar. Only I can dismiss my Darbar—for I am the King. From today, you are not my friend.

(*And he strikes his right thumb nail to his upper teeth to convey that they are no longer friends.*)

RANI:   No, my boy.

DALIP:   And he doesn't go on *shikar* with me any more, Mai. I'm going to make Baba write to his London Queen to change him. *I* shall sign the letter, and the Queen will do as I say—for I am the King, and Queens listen only to Kings.

RANI:   No, my boy.

LAWRENCE:   Your Highness . . .

DALIP:   (*Interrupting, with the same gesture.*) Go! (*Exit.*)

RANI:   What are you going to do to him?

LAWRENCE:   He's perfectly safe. He's going to Simla.

RANI:   Shame! Larins, after all you told me. You're dirty and cruel! How can you snatch my son away from me? For eight months I kept him in my womb. Then I brought him up slowly with care and love. What will I do if anything happens to him? He gets frightened, you know. He has no one except me. Who will look after him? I don't need a kingdom, but don't take my son away.

(*Long pause. Suddenly excited she goes closer to him.*)

Larins, I've an idea. Why don't you take us to England? Let's leave this dirty place to the Angrez. Come.

(*Lawrence shakes his head.*)

Why, what's the matter? All right then we can go to Nepal.

LAWRENCE:   No.

RANI:   (*Broken.*) Oh Larins! I don't want to go away. Larins, I love you. (*Leaving.*)

I'll always think of you. You too, remember me. (*Trying to smile.*) Adieu, said the Queen.

LAWRENCE:   Adieu, said her Resident.

(*Exit Rani. Lawrence moves towards stage right. Whispering offstage. Commotion. Sounds become louder. Muffled shouts 'The Rani is banished,' 'The Mother of the Khalsa is leaving,' 'Save the Punjab.' Bells, confusion, music. Full lights, and Sher Singh bursts in.*)

SHER SINGH:   Ranjit Singh is dead today!

LAWRENCE:   Why?

SHER SINGH:   The Punjab is dead today!

LAWRENCE:   Why, my friend?

SHER SINGH:   You've banished the Mother of the Punjab. Time is up. His Highness is too young to know what he wants. The Punjab is now another pawn in the Angrez's game.

LAWRENCE:   Sher Singh . . .

SHER SINGH:   (*Interrupting.*) I want to resign, sir. I too want to go away. I'm tired of this place.

LAWRENCE:   Don't be a fool, Sher Singh. This is political life. There are ups and there are downs.

SHER SINGH:   Not when your Mother's banished.

LAWRENCE:   I didn't know you felt so strongly about her.

SHER SINGH:   She's the Mother of the Punjab.

LAWRENCE:   A tough Sardar like you believes in these myths?

SHER SINGH:   She's flesh and blood. You're separating her from her son. The Angrez is clever. He needs the boy for legitimacy; and the mother is thrown out.

LAWRENCE:    But these separations take place.

SHER SINGH:    Larins Sahib, in our land the relationship between mother and son is sacred.

LAWRENCE:    So many young soldiers die. They get separated from their mothers.

SHER SINGH:    They die in battle—a noble death.

LAWRENCE:    This is also battle.

SHER SINGH:    No. She's Ranjit Singh's wife. And the Angrez have insulted the Punjab.

LAWRENCE:    There are reasons of state policy, Sher Singh.

SHER SINGH:    She was the Queen, wasn't she?

LAWRENCE:    There are queens and queens.

SHER SINGH:    No, there is a way of treating a Queen. I have tasted enough English brandy. Now I must go. Time is up.

LAWRENCE:    Stay, Sher Singh. Did you know her?

SHER SINGH:    You knew her.

LAWRENCE:    She wan't the most exemplary ruler.

SHER SINGH:    You should say that, sir? I thought you respected her.

LAWRENCE:    I do. I do, Sher Singh.

SHER SINGH:    I thought she was your special friend.

LAWRENCE:    She was.

SHER SINGH:    Then why did you do it?

LAWRENCE:    I am executing my government's policy.

(*Pause.*)

SHER SINGH:    You hypocrite! You never loved anyone. You don't deserve anyone's friendship. You turned into a hypocrite when you saw how powerful you'd become. You imagined that you had become Ranjit Singh.

LAWRENCE:    (*Shouting.*) Stop it. Do you know to whom you are talking?

SHER SINGH:    To a friend, who was . . .

LAWRENCE:    No. You are talking to the Angrez Badshah!

SHER SINGH:    Your Angrez Badshahs, your *chogahs*, your jewels, purple cushions—they were signals. I understand you now! You're evil. (*Laughs bitterly.*) You still think you're doing it for the Punjab—as though . . . as though nothing had happened. If you realized it, I'd call you ambitious. Not evil. But you don't know yourself and that terrifies me.

LAWRENCE:    Stop it! Stop it!

SHER SINGH:    (*Quietly.*) I thought we were friends. We have nothing more
to say to each other. I might as well go.

LAWRENCE:    Stay, Sher Singh.

(*Pause.*)

SHER SINGH:    (*Quietly.*) Did you banish the Rani because Dalip insulted
your government today?

LAWRENCE:    No.

SHER SINGH:    Yes. You were looking for an excuse to do this, and today's
incident gave you that excuse.

LAWRENCE:    No, no.

SHER SINGH:    Then why did you do it?

(*No reply.*)

I know. Reasons of state policy.

(*Pause. Looks at Lawrence, who remains silent.*)

But they can be met if one believes in oneself.

LAWRENCE:    Perhaps one has stopped believing in oneself.

SHER SINGH:    That's not true, sir. It's a matter of choice. You've chosen.
You could have chosen the way of the heart. Because she was
your friend—you won't deny that? Or you could have chosen to
obey your country's order. Your duty to her or your duty to *your* Queen.
You've chosen. In my terms, Larins Sahib, it's a choice between
the Punjab and England. Your Queen and my Queen. That's where
we part. I won't have anything to do with the Company Raj.
Farewell!

LAWRENCE:    Stay, my friend. Stay, Sher Singh.

SHER SINGH:    I feel sad now. For you were our hope—our golden evening.
You gave us a sense of life—to me, to the Rani, to Dalip. We returned
it with the only thing we had: our love. But we were mistaken.

LAWRENCE:    Everything isn't lost. The Punjab is still there. Together we'll
make it into a rich, prosperous land. Together we'll make it shine like
the sun. The Jats, the Sikhs, the Paharis, the Pathans—they depend on
you and me. You can't leave it all half done. Remember what you
promised me in Delhi.

SHER SINGH:    Yes.

LAWRENCE:    You said the One-eyed Lion would be proud of us.

SHER SINGH:    But I didn't think you'd start acting like him.

(*Suddenly becomes embarrassed.*)

LAWRENCE:    (*Barking.*) What do you mean?

SHER SINGH:  (*Embarrassed.*) No, nothing.

    (*Pause.*)

LAWRENCE:  (*Softly.*) Do you think what I did was dishonourable?

SHER SINGH:  Why bother with empty words? One of our wise men has said: 'Honour is only what you think other people think of you, and the attention you pay to their opinions.' We've chosen. You've chosen to serve the British Raj. I've chosen to serve the Punjab. We're now in opposite camps.

LAWRENCE:  We're still friends.

SHER SINGH:  What's friendship to do with it? Anybody can be friends. When my Rani is heartbroken, you talk of honour and friendship.

    (*Pause, Lawrence silent.*)

Farewell, Larins Sahib. Before I leave, let me tell you: I shall return. When I do, I shall be on the other side. I shall come to avenge my Queen. I shall be armed and the whole Punjab army will be behind me. The Angrez will be thrown out of the Punjab or I shall die. Larins Sahib, you've made a man of me, and I thank you. It was another Sher Singh who wanted to be an English gentleman. He's as dead as the One-eyed Lion. You taught me the magic of the Lion' name, Larins Sahib. Now I shall go from village to village, from house to house, and shout his name. I shall shout (*and he shouts.*)

'Come on men. Take your swords. Remember the Lion, and save your land.' I shall rally every son and father. We shall kick out the Angrez. And we shall save our land. Farewell, Larins Sahib, we shall meet on the battlefield again.

    (*Exit. Long pause. Lawrence initially looks dejected. He collects himself slowly takes a deep breath, raising himself to his full height. A glow returns to his face. Goes to the mirror again, and adjusts his chogah. Then he swaggers about, displaying his jewel, triumphantly. Sound of footsteps.*)

LAWRENCE:  (*Authoritatively.*) Who's there?

    (*Enter Edwardes.*)

EDWARDES:  I've been looking for you, sir.

LAWRENCE:  What is it?

EDWARDES:  Special dak from Calcutta, sir.

LAWRENCE:  (*Impatiently.*) Later!

EDWARDES:  It's come by special messenger, sir. From the Governor-General.

LAWRENCE:  Later! Did you see Sher Singh leaving?

EDWARDES:   (*Puzzled.*) Yes, sir. I meant to ask you. He looked upset, and he walked past me without even recognizing me.

LAWRENCE:   (*With an effort.*) He's leaving us. Leaving permanently.

EDWARDES:   I'm sorry to hear it.

LAWRENCE:   (*More to himself.*) But I still have the Punjab. Let them go away. I don't need them. I don't need the Rani; nor Sher Singh. I have the Punjab. Angrez Badshah! The new Lion is here. I am the Punjab!

EDWARDES:   (*Uncomfortably.*) Yes, sir. The messenger is waiting.

LAWRENCE:   What is it?

EDWARDES:   (*Producing a sealed letter.*) It's marked 'personal and confidential,' sir.

LAWRENCE:   Open it.

(*Edwardes tears the seal.*)

Read it.

EDWARDES:   (*Delicately.*) But it's personal, sir.

LAWRENCE:   Read it.

EDWARDES:   (*Reading.*) My dear Lawrence, I regret to inform you that the Court of Directors of the Company are persuaded that the Government of India no longer requires your services in the Punjab. Mr Currie will temporarily assume charge at Lahore until a suitable successor is appointed. He will prepare grounds for the formal annexation of the Punjab. You are requested to proceed to Calcutta.'

(*Long silence.*)

LAWRENCE:   You'd better go now, Edwardes. I'll take off the Lion's *chogah*. It's grown too hot for me.

(*Long pause. Takes off the chogah slowly. Lights fade.*)

# Afterword

The major characters in this play existed. Its action is based on events in the Punjab in 1846–7, and was reconstructed from documents and letters exchanged by the principal characters. The historically curious may be interested to know what subsequently became of these characters.

Henry Lawrence was transferred to Rajasthan from the Punjab: a demotion in the eyes of his contemporaries. His younger brother, John Lawrence (mentioned in Act I), succeeded him in the Punjab and rose brilliantly to become the famous Lord Lawrence, the Governor-General and Viceroy of India. Henry Lawrence flickered once more briefly into history when he died defending the Residency in Lucknow in the 1857 Mutiny. Much was made at the time of his heroism; some even said that he had saved the British Empire.

That he saved the British Empire was in a sense true, though not in the way most people believed. The British won the 1857 war mainly through the support of the Punjab troops. The loyalty of the Punjab had been won ten years before by Henry Lawrence through his 'rule' of justice and generosity. Even today people talk about him in many villages of the Punjab.

Rani Jindan escaped from the Sheikhupura jail. She was seized and banished from the Punjab to a fortress in Benares. Once again she escaped, this time to Nepal where the king gave her asylum. She was never allowed to return to India nor to see her son, till the very end of her life—after sixteen years—in May 1863. She died three months later. Dalip scattered her ashes from the banks of the river in Nasik because he was not allowed to enter the Punjab. She had wished them thrown into the Ravi, near Lahore.

Sher Singh, true to his word, returned to throw out the Angrez from the Punjab. He rallied a sizeable force and launched such a successful attack on the British that the frightened establishment in Calcutta had to call in British troops from all over India to fight essentially one man in what historically came to be called the Second Sikh War. Sher Singh fought gallantly, but it was an unequal contest. With his defeat the spirit of Ranjit Singh finally died in the Punjab and the British formally annexed it in 1849. However, for the Punjabis, Sher Singh had salvaged the honour they had lost in Sobraon; and they were thankful to him.

Dalip was converted to Christianity and sent to England as a young boy where the British Government gave him an annual pension and the Elvedon Estate in Sussex. He grew up a dandy—mildly ostentations, favouring black velvet jackets (he was affectionately called the 'Black Prince')—and was rumoured to be a great favourite of Queen Victoria for many years. He married a German Ethiopian girl, Bamba Muller, who gave him two sons and three daughters. But he lived far beyond his means and ran up large debts.

In his later years, he realized he had been cheated by the British and, reverting to Sikhism, made a ludicrous effort to enlist the help of European powers and Indian Princes to win back his kingdom. He called himself an 'implacable foe' of the British people. His efforts, however, did not come to much and he spent his last years frustrated and angry. He died in Paris in 1893 of paralysis, and was buried a week later at Elvedon.

# *Mira*

❦

*Mira* was first performed at the La Mama Theater, New York, on 20 May 1970. It was directed by Martin Brenzell, with original music by David Walker, and the following cast:

| | |
|---|---|
| Yolande Bavan | Mira |
| Patricia Conway | Uda |
| Farid Farrah | Jai |
| Gretchen Oehler | Jhali |
| Erik Robinson | Rana |
| Thomas Aronis | Percussion, harp and harmonium |
| John Littlefield | Flutes |

Note: The running time of the La Mama production was 90 minutes.

*The play has since been performed in Mexico City (1971), Bombay (1972), New Delhi (1973 and 1998), Ahmedabad (1973), Madras (1985) and a number of other cities. It was first published in Spanish (Mira: Rito de Krishna, translated by Enrique Hett, Institute Nacional de Bellas Artes, Mexico, D.F., 1971).*

# Characters

ACTRESS 1    (Mira)

ACTOR 1      (Rana)

ACTOR 2      (Jai)

ACTRESS 2    (Uda)

ACTRESS 3    (Jhali)

*The action of the play takes place in early sixteenth century Mewar, a princely state in North-western India.*

# Note

The play is in one act to be performed in one sitting. All actors are on stage all the time; there are no exits or entrances. When actors speak their stage directions, they do not generally enact what they say. Action does not stop when a dance is indicated—the dialogue continues throughout the dance, as a visual and emotional aid to the actors' words.

It is best to use Mira's original songs. The best translation is by Shama Futehally (*In the Dark of the Heart: Songs of Meera*, Harper Collins, New York, 1994) from the original by Deshrajsinh Bhati, *Mirabai aur unki Padavali*, Ashok Prakashan, Delhi, 1962.

# 1. The Prologue

ACTRESS 1:    I am Mira. I am an ant on a matchstick lit at both ends.

ALL:    (*Chanting.*) I sing to the hearts of men and women; I dance before him, and I wail of the divine death.

ACTRESS 1:    (*Sings.*) 'Mira,' he said, 'sing.'

                    'I will,' I said, 'if you play the flute'

                    'Mira,' he said, 'sing, sing'

                    And he set the whole universe humming.

ALL:    (*Chanting.*) They sing my songs; and remember their sons.

ACTRESS 1:    I never had a son.

ACTOR 2:    It's the difference between knowing and being good.

ACTOR 1:    To know is to know yourself; to be good is to love another.

ACTRESS 1:    I love my god.

ACTOR 2:    What about the Rana?

ACTRESS 1:    What about my pain?

ACTRESS 3:    For centuries they have been singing her songs.

ACTRESS 1:    A tiger dies and leaves his skin behind;

                a man dies and leaves his name behind.

ACTOR 2:    It's been glory. A saint—what more does she want?

ACTRESS 1:    And the ones who thought I was barren?

ACTRESS 2:    She ruined this fertile land.

ACTRESS 1:    Blood flowed in our rivers.

ACTRESS 3:    Mother's milk flowed in our rivers.

ACTRESS 1:    This mother is dry.

ACTRESS 2:    The land is wasted and poor.

ACTRESS 1:    Don't shoot at a sparrow; you will only spoil a good arrow.

ACTOR 2:    What more does she want?

ACTRESS 1:    You are only delaying the story. It is the day of my marriage.

     (*The dance of the marriage ceremony.*)

# 2. Isn't the Bed Small for the Two of Us?

ACTRESS 1:   It is the night of my marriage.

ACTOR 1:   The Rana and Mira walk in with candles. The Rana places his candle on a holder.

ACTRESS 1:   Mira nervous, looks around the room in awe.

ACTRESS 3:   The pace of this scene is slow, hesitant; long pauses and embarrassed silences.

ACTRESS 2:   The mood is soft and tender, to grasp the undercurrent of desire and the nuances of a situation where physical touch precedes and leads to emotional contact.

ACTOR 1:   The Rana picks up a flower from the bed and gives it to her.

ACTRESS 1:   Which increases her embarrassment.

ACTOR 1:   Then he leads her before the wooden image of Kali, which is chiselled on the door.

ACTOR 1:   Bow to Mother!

ACTRESS 1:   She hesitates.

ACTOR 1:   Bow to her. Kali is our family goddess.

ACTRESS 1:   I don't like her face.

ACTOR 1:   What?

ACTRESS 1:   Mira is frightened.

ACTOR 1:   Don't be afraid. A cat holds a mouse and her kitten in the same teeth. Only our enemies are afraid of her.

ACTRESS 1:   If it will catch mice why not have a squirrel instead of a cat.

ACTOR 1:   Kali will give you a son if you worship her.

ACTRESS 1:   They say parenthesis it is painful when the son comes out.

ACTOR 1:   Rana goes back to bed, and slowly begins to undress. Embarrassed pause.

   (Dance of the bed.)

ACTRESS 1:   Isn't the bed small for the two of us?

ACTOR 1:   No.

ACTRESS 1:   In my father's home they always gave me a big bed to sleep in. Don't you have enough beds in the palace?

ACTOR 1:   Yes.

ACTRESS 1:   Will I have one for myself later on?

ACTOR 1:    You are the Rana's wife.

ACTRESS 1:    Yes?

ACTOR 1:    Don't you know what that means?

ACTRESS 1:    Oh, yes.

ACTOR 1:    What?

ACTRESS 1:    Oh yes . . . yes I do.

ACTOR 1:    Women are instructed by nature what men have to learn from books.

ACTRESS 1:    A vessel is filled slowly by falling drops of rain.

ACTOR 1:    We will make a son for the kingdom.

ACTRESS 1:    A son comes to those who have earned him.

ACTOR 1:    The son will make war and rule the world.

ACTRESS 1:    A son will be born out of love.

ACTOR 1:    The Rana is walking about uncomfortably. Now he hesitantly gets into the bed.

ACTRESS 1:    Mira looks the other way.

ACTOR 1:    The poet says, every month the moon vainly tries to match Mira's face. Having failed, it destroys its work and begins again.

ACTRESS 1:    Even honey falling on a roof of sugar blushes at the Rana's words.

ACTOR 1:    Is Mira going to sleep like this? . . . I am looking the other way. . . . I am going to turn around. . . . Are you going to sleep like this?

ACTRESS 1:    I am not sleepy.

ACTOR 1:    Come.

ACTRESS 1:    The Rana should sleep. . . . Shall I blow out the candle?

ACTOR 1:    Mira will be cold outside.

ACTRESS 1:    Is the Rana pleased?

ACTRESS 3:    The poet says, 'You are fortunate, dear friends, that you can tell what happened with your lovers, the jests and laughter, all the words and joys; after my sweetheart put his hand to the knot of my dress, I swear that I remember nothing.'

# 3. The Rainbird

❦

ACTOR 2: (*Sings.*) So began Mira's life in her new home, her husband's home. Days passed into months and the prince and the princess were happy. Any day of the year they could be found playing in the gardens Catching butterflies, singing with myna birds, resting under the Ashok tree and looking into each others eyes.

After some time, the prince tired of this sport; he was reminded of his duties to the state and his people. And Mira had more and more time to herself.

ACTRESS 1: A year later. Mira enters into an empty courtyard.

ACTRESS 3: And discovers Jhali, her faithful servant, waiting for her.

ACTRESS 1: I'm here! Isn't anybody home? Are you all dead? Oh it's you?

ACTRESS 3: Who did you expect to find—a guard of honour?

ACTRESS 1: If that's how I'm welcomed, I might as well go back.

ACTRESS 3: You've only been away an afternoon.

ACTRESS 1: I went away for ever.

ACTRESS 3: You were angry.

ACTRESS 1: I was going to die.

ACTRESS 3: So what happened?

ACTRESS 1: I . . . I got scared.

ACTRESS 3: The doctor's advice to the lovesick is: first drink the nectar from his lips; then follow it up with his warm hand on your breasts; cap it with a soothing massage of your loins and hips.

ACTRESS 1: Mira is angry with the Rana.

ACTRESS 3: Marriage without quarrel is like food without spice.

ACTRESS 1: Marriage without love is no food at all.

ACTRESS 3: He can't play with you forever. The Rana must rule the kingdom.

ACTRESS 1: The Rana must also rule the Rani. He only thinks about the kingdom.

ACTRESS 3: Mira only thinks of love.

ACTRESS 1: He only thinks of war.

ACTRESS 3: He is a conqueror.

ACTRESS 1: The real conqueror first overcomes himself.

ACTRESS 3: He is a soldier.

ACTRESS 1: The best soldiers are not warlike.

(*Dance of the rainbird.*)

ACTRESS 1:    I saw a rainbird today, Jhali. It was noon and hot, not a cloud in the sky, not a breeze everything was parched dry. Even the leaves bristled painfully when you walked on them.

ACTRESS 3:    Were you barefoot?

ACTRESS 1:    And what do I see . . . this rainbird in the sky crying in anguish. It was dying of thirst.

ACTRESS 3:    The heron is a saint as long as there's no fish in sight.

ACTRESS 1:    It came near the lake and I thought I heard it sigh with relief. The crying stopped. With shining eyes it dove down, but just as it was about to hit the water it leaped up again and went higher and higher into the heavens, into the sky—away from temptation. Even if it's dying of thirst, the rainbird only drinks rain.

ACTRESS 3:    The tiger who waited for the jungle to bring him food starved, I think.

(*The procession of the demons.*)

ACTRESS 2:    Enter Uda, the Rana's sister.

What are these?

ACTRESS 1:    Flowers. I picked them myself.

ACTRESS 2:    (*Throwing them.*) There!

ACTRESS 1:    She threw my flowers away.

ACTRESS 2:    You know I can't stand wild flowers. It was tiresome enough going through all your clothes this morning and throwing out the yellow colours.

ACTRESS 1:    You didn't! She threw my clothes away.

ACTRESS 2:    When are you going to give us a son?

ACTRESS 1:    He has to love me, for me to give him a son. A single lamp, no matter how bright, always casts a shadow. Put another one beside it and the darkness of both disappears.

ACTRESS 2:    You have been married over a year and people are asking questions. A princess marries to give a son; only a widow marries to please herself.

ACTRESS 1:    She has a face like a moon and a heart of poison.

ACTRESS 3:    Always suspect the sister-in-law who is too fond of the bride.

ACTRESS 1:    When sitting she is a cat; when springing she is a tiger.

ACTRESS 3:    Women are instructed by nature; men have to learn from books.

ACTRESS 1:    It takes two to make a son. The chariot can't go anywhere on a single wheel.

# 4. You'll Sleep Better Upstairs

ACTRESS 2: Sound of footsteps in the distance.

ACTRESS 1: Mira suddenly nervous.

Jhali, it's he. Quick, go away. No, come here. My hair isn't even combed. And my forehead is naked. Oh . . .

ACTRESS 3: If you spent your time sensibly, we wouldn't have these panics. Instead you go skipping around the lake, playing with your birds, and god knows what in the burning sun and making a scandal of . . .

ACTRESS 1: Are there any flowers for my hair? Oh, she threw them away. Quick, how do I look?

ACTRESS 3: Oh, you look pretty.

ACTRESS 1: Now go away. Wait. Am I pretty?

ACTRESS 3: Yes.

ACTRESS 2: Rana enters from the other side.

ACTRESS 3: Softer colours to feel gentler mood.

ALL: Mira blushing.

ACTRESS 1: Rana!

ALL: The Rana is inebriated.

ACTOR 1: Mira!

ALL: Mira shyly.

ACTRESS 1: The Rana has no time for Mira anymore?

ALL: Rana defensively.

ACTOR 1: The Rana has been in the council of war.

ALL: Affectionately.

ACTOR 1: Where has Mira been today?

ALL: Confused pause.

ACTRESS 1: After the Rana said those things this morning . . . I went to the lake.

ALL: Rana smiling.

ACTOR 1: To drown yourself.

ALL: Tenderly, clasping her.

ACTOR 1: Oh my Mira, my Mira.

ALL: Snuggling upto him.

ACTRESS 1:   How is the Rana?

ACTOR 1:   Drunk!

    (*The Dance of Kali.*)

ACTOR 1:   Did Mira go to Kali's temple today?

ACTRESS 1:   No.

ACTOR 1:   Then Mother hasn't been fed again today.

ACTRESS 1:   No.

ACTOR 1:   What if somebody didn't feed Mira?

ACTRESS 1:   I can't feed blood to her.

ACTOR 1:   It's only a goat's blood. It isn't human blood.

ACTRESS 1:   Can't someone else feed her?

ACTOR 1:   Only the Rana's wife feeds Kali. She will give us a son if she is fed and happy.

ACTRESS 1:   Can't we give her milk?

ACTOR 1:   Don't you want to give us a son?

ACTRESS 3:   The chariot can't go anywhere on a single wheel.

ACTOR 2:   Are young fish taught to swim?

ACTRESS 3:   Thirst isn't quenched by shouting water.

ACTOR 2:   The mouth isn't burnt by pronouncing fire.

ACTRESS 1:   Love that destroys the distinction between the lover, the beloved and love is to be practised.

ACTOR 2:   The nature of love can't be expressed.

ACTRESS 1:   A body without love is dead.

ACTRESS 2:   The little fish splashes in even a mouthful of water.

    (*Dance of the chained captive.*)

ACTOR 1:   The Rana is sleepy now.

ACTRESS 1:   Shall I help you up?

ACTOR 1:   No.

ACTRESS 1:   I was wondering—that is, I was wondering if I could get anything.

ACTOR 1:   Nothing.

ACTRESS 1:   Rana . . .?

ACTOR 1:   I want to sleep.

ACTRESS 1:   I could help you upstairs. You will sleep better there.

ACTOR 1:   No.

ACTRESS 1:   I'll put you to sleep, Rana. Come.

ACTOR 1:   Oh, Mira, why won't you let me sleep?

ACTRESS 1:   You'll sleep better upstairs.

ACTOR 1:    We are all right here.

ACTRESS 1:    Let's go upstairs. Then I can also be with you.

ACTOR 1:    I don't want anyone with me—I just want to sleep. Mira, the Rana is tired. He has to prepare for war.

ACTRESS 1:    Mira will massage the Rana. Does the Rana care for Mira?

ACTOR 1:    Yes.

ACTRESS 1:    Mira's heart is like a horse on an open plain—easily let loose but hard to restrain.

ACTOR 1:    The Rana has to fight a war.

ACTRESS 1:    The best soldiers are not warlike.

# 5. There is Blood on My Hands

ACTRESS 1:    A few weeks later. Mira sings to herself as she bathes Krishna.
(*Song of the River.*)

ACTRESS 2:    Enter Uda.
Scrub it well. It's dirty all over.

ACTRESS 1:    I bathe him every day.

ACTRESS 2:    Though he washes three times a day will a crow become a crane? (*Snatching it.*)
Aren't you too old to be playing with dolls?

ACTRESS 1:    Give him back to me!

ACTRESS 2:    (*Returning it.*) It's so ordinary looking.

ACTRESS 1:    He is not ordinary.
(*Dance of the golden calf.*)

ACTRESS 2:    Mira, since you won't visit her temple, we have brought Mother to you. Kali is strong on the blood of ten thousand generations of goats. She leads our armies in war. She gives life; she takes life. She is time.

ACTRESS 1:    Oh no! She is death!

ACTRESS 2:    She is birth, and rebirth. Kneel before Kali, pray to her for a son, and make this humble offering of holy blood.

ACTOR 1:    O holy goddess of million wars, give us victory!

ACTRESS 1:    I don't want war.

ACTRESS 2:    O holy goddess of million children, may the line of Ranas forever live!

ACTRESS 1:    It is painful when the son comes out.

ACTRESS 2:    O holy goddess, bless our house with happiness.

ACTRESS 1:    I don't want to be happy.
(*Chant to Kali.*)

ACTOR 2:    My heart is a burning ground,
For you Dark One.

ACTOR 1:    Dance your eternal dance, Mother,
My heart wishes nothing more.

ACTRESS 3:    Burn forever the funeral,
Scatter the ashes of the dead.

ACTRESS 2:    Death conquering Time is your anklet,
              Come dance your rhythms, Mother.

ALL:    That I may see you inside my closed eye.

ACTRESS 1:    Death says come; life says go. I want to go; I don't want to
              come.

ACTOR 2:    Uda forcibly places the vessel in her hands. Mira looks at the
            blood and faints. The blood spills on the floor as the vessel comes
            down with a crash.

            (*The dance of the slaughter-house.*)

ACTRESS 3:    Every tree has bark.

ACTOR 1:    Mira, Mira!

ACTRESS 3:    When you spit at the moon it falls back on you.

ACTRESS 2:    What is more illusory than the fire of a glow worm?

ACTOR 2:    She is recovering.

ACTRESS 1:    There is blood on my hands. Blood on my clothes. Blood on
              the ground!

ACTOR 1:    (*Echo*) Mira, Mira.

ACTRESS 1:    It's hot all over.

            (*Echo*)

Mira, Mira.

ACTRESS 1:    The sun shines on the desert.

            (*Echo*)

Who is that woman in white with tiger's teeth and blood in her hands?

            (*Echo*)

Who is that woman with her smug high forehead and her hungry
butcher's eyes.

            (*Echo*)

I don't like women with strangler's hands.

            (*Echo*)

He didn't want to die.

            (*Echo*)

He was afraid when she killed him.

ACTRESS 3:    Mira, try to understand others.

ACTRESS 1:    When I'm old and understanding like you, I shall also look
              the other way when I see evil. Now I am young . . .

ACTRESS 2:    There is evil in the house. Kali is in pain.

            (*Hide and seek dance.*)

ACTOR 1:    Rana begins to withdraw.

ACTRESS 1:    Mira attempts to hold him.

ACTOR 1:    Only Mira can save us.

ACTRESS 1:    I can't do it.

ACTOR 1:    There will be no heir to the throne.

ACTRESS 1:    Rana, don't ask me to do it.

ACTOR 1:    Mira, when a dog barks at a mountain, who gets hurt, the dog or the mountain?

ACTRESS 1:    I will do anything for you. I live for you. But not this. If I did, I'd stop being Mira. I am being asked to play the actor who is elevated from peasant to king for two hours.

# 6. Enter Jai

✼

(*Dance of the Warrior Prince.*)

ALL:   (*Chant.*) Sound of drum and voice of trumpet
             and the horse's joyful cry
             Stately as a golden palm
             Now the warlike Prince has come.
             Blessed with all manly virtues
             Lion-like in build and muscle
             Warrior Jaimal pious-hearted
             Forth he brings the wheat and treasure.
             Warlike leader of his forces
             Like the all-consuming fire
             Jai by his graceful mein
             Joyful makes the proud Rana.

ACTOR 2:   Enter Jai.

ACTRESS 2:   To sounds of shouts, cheers, bells.

ACTOR 1:   Rana comes forward.

ACTOR 2:   Jai bows.

ACTOR 1:   Rana returns the bow.

ACTRESS 2:   And the two embrace.

ACTOR 1:   Mewar has waited many moons to welcome the noble Prince.

ACTOR 2:   To be in the sacred presence of unvanquished Mewar is high honour.
And he bows again.

ACTOR 1:   The Rana again returns Jai's bow and takes his arm and leads him before Kali.

ACTOR 2:   Jai bows to Kali's image.

ACTOR 1:   Rana then leads Jai to his sister and introduces them with elaborate ritual as demanded by the occasion.

ACTOR 1:   Our sister, Suryavanshi, pearl of the sun race, the Sisodia princess, Udabai.

ACTOR 2:   Jai bows even more elaborately.

ACTRESS 2:   She covers her head with her *ordny*, which hides her face as well—a mark of modesty and acknowledgement.

ACTOR 2:    May the sun forever give strength to Sisodia!

ACTOR 1:    The Rana next leads Jai to Mira.

ACTOR 2:    Jai again bows ceremoniously.

ACTRESS 2:    The great amount of ritual and style that has so far attached to this scene abruptly comes to an end.

ACTRESS 1:    As Mira, instead of courtesying ritually, leaps up with a spontaneous and joyful cry.

(*Carousel dance.*)

ACTRESS 1:    Jai!

For a moment she stares at him; then springs up and runs up to him. Jai, oh Jai! Jai for victory.

She begins to speak with feverish vivacity as if she feared that she would stop and think. She holds him in a spontaneous embrace.

Let me look at you cousin. How handsome you've become! No, no, don't look at me. Are these new clothes? You're so good-looking in them.

ACTOR 2:    Jai laughs.

ACTRESS 1:    She embraces him again.

Oh Jai, Jai for victory! I've been expecting you for so long. Rana said you were to come a month ago. I thought you'd never come. Let me look at you again.

She laughs and pulls his cheek playfully.

ACTOR 2:    He blushes self-consciously and tries to extricate himself from Mira's unorthodox welcome.

(*Dance of the Marionettes.*)

ACTRESS 1:    Jai, what's happened to your tongue? Say something.

ACTOR 2:    Those who speak don't know, those who know don't speak.

ACTOR 1:    The noble Jai has come to lead the alliance against the Mughal.

ACTOR 2:    Not lead, but fight together under the leadership of the great House of Mewar.

ACTOR 1:    He has brought twenty-thousand of the finest horses of Marwar.

ACTRESS 1:    The best riders fall the hardest.

ACTRESS 2:    A noble commander must have a noble army.

ACTOR 2:    The fruit seller's mangoes are always sweet.

ACTRESS 2:    Surely they must be the sweetest if this fruit seller is any guide.

ACTOR 1:    The Mughal is rushing down like a river, and nothing will stop him.

ACTOR 2:    The Rajput princes will damn the river.

ACTOR 1:    The real soldier only speaks of success.

ACTRESS 1:   I'd rather be a peasant in peace than a prince in war.

ACTOR 2:    This will be a good war.

ACTRESS 1:   There is never a good war.

ACTOR 1:    There must be a war against the Mughal.

ACTOR 2:    Ride a horse to catch a horse.

ACTRESS 2:   To catch the Mughal is to catch a fox.

ACTRESS 1:   Only cats know cats.

ACTOR 1:    We have to fight to defend our honour.

ACTRESS 1:   The bird chooses its tree, not the tree the bird.

ACTRESS 2:   Our men aren't afraid to fight.

ACTOR 2:    True gold isn't afraid of fire.

ACTRESS 1:   The best soldiers are not warlike.

ACTOR 2:    He who leads an ox to drink has to get wet.

ACTRESS 1:   War is the festival of death.

# 7. The Sister-in-law is Jealous

ACTRESS 2: If the Rani pleases, a Rana's wife doesn't carry on in this manner.

ACTRESS 1: Mira puzzled.

ACTRESS 2: She doesn't observe the looks of young men. She sees her lord's image in every man.

ACTRESS 1: How can I see the Rana in every man? The Rana is too good.

ACTRESS 2: There are ways which must be observed in court.

ACTRESS 1: Mira questioningly.

ACTRESS 2: It was evident to the smallest child.

ACTRESS 1: Mira still puzzled.

ACTRESS 2: There is a way of welcoming guests.

ACTRESS 1: Mira courtesying in an exaggerated way.
Oh, you mean like this?
And she smiles.

ACTRESS 2: Yes.

ACTRESS 1: But he's my cousin.

ACTRESS 2: You don't go up and embrace a man like that. I almost died of shame. Think of your sacred husband. What must he have felt . . . and in front of everyone . . . if I had been the Rani . . .

ACTRESS 1: Oh, I didn't mean . . . I didn't mean . . . I didn't think the Rana would . . . What shall I do? What will the Rana think?

ACTRESS 2: The damage is done.

ACTRESS 1: Appealing.
What am I going to do?

ACTRESS 2: You will stay away from your cousin. At least the court will not get any more ideas.

ACTRESS 1: What about the Rana?

ACTOR 1: Enter Rana.

ACTRESS 1: Mira blushes and leaves.

ACTOR 1: Why did Mira leave in such a hurry? Her cousin was asking for her.

ACTRESS 2: Already?

ACTOR 1: The Rana looking surprised.

ACTRESS 2:   A wise man drapes a curtain between a stranger and his mistress.

ACTOR 1:   Jai is a fine young man.

ACTRESS 2:   Even an elephant may slip.

ACTOR 1:   Oil your own wheel first.

ACTRESS 2:   The heron is a saint as long as there's no fish in sight.

ACTOR 1:   It is for the Rana to judge the Rani.

ACTRESS 2:   A king is supposed to see by his ears.

ACTOR 1:   Why doesn't Princess Uda make friends with Mira?

ACTRESS 2:   Mira has everything and she doesn't want to be a Rani.

ACTOR 1:   Uda would like to be Rani, wouldn't she?

ACTRESS 2:   Uda is quiet.

ACTOR 1:   Uda would like to be a Rani, wouldn't she?

ACTRESS 2:   Uda nods.

ACTOR 1:   The Rana leaves.

ACTRESS 2:   Uda sees Jai and Mira coming. Hides.

# 8. Surely the Rana Knows

❦

ACTOR 2:   Mira is the Rani of a magnificent palace!

ACTRESS 1:   Where palaces are magnificent, fields are poor and granaries are empty.

ACTOR 2:   Something is wrong, and I'm afraid.

ACTRESS 1:   Nothing is wrong.

ACTOR 2:   Something is wrong.

ACTRESS 1:   Jai, I'm going to have a son.

ACTOR 2:   Jai claps in approval.

ACTRESS 1:   Shh . . . not so loud. No one is supposed to know.

ACTOR 2:   Surely the Rana knows.

ACTRESS 1:   No. Especially not he.

ACTOR 2:   I am so proud. We should announce it to the whole world.

ACTRESS 1:   Oh no!

ACTOR 2:   How do you know it's a boy?

ACTRESS 1:   I feel it inside me.

And she places his hand on her stomach.

ACTOR 2:   I can't feel anything.

ACTRESS 1:   I can.

ACTOR 2 and ACTRESS 1:   They stare at each other.

ACTOR 2:   Then Jai smiles.

ACTRESS 1:   She smiles back.

ACTOR 2:   And Jai embraces her.

I am so happy.

ACTRESS 1:   Happy, happy.

ACTOR 2:   What are you going to call the child?

ACTRESS 1:   Son.

ACTOR 2:   What if it's a girl?

ACTRESS 1:   I'm going to have a son.

ACTOR 2:   What will be his name?

ACTRESS 1:   The son.

ACTOR 2:   Jai takes her hand affectionately.

ACTRESS 1 AND ACTOR 2:   And both excitedly dance to beautiful music.

ACTOR 2:   Enter Rana.

ACTRESS 2:   And Uda.

ACTRESS 3:   And Jhali.

ACTOR 1:   Let us drink to the alliance.

ACTOR 2:   To victory!

     (*Dance of the warriors.*)

ACTOR 1:   To victory! The Mughal fox has crossed the river and tripled his strength.

ACTOR 2:   Why didn't the governors resist?

ACTOR 1:   They are stooges of an infidel dynasty. The blood of Ghengiz Khan and Tamerlane rushes through Babur's veins.

ACTOR 2:   The blood of Babur will pale before the Rajput alliance.

ACTRESS 2:   A shrewd commander doesn't underrate an enemy.

ACTOR 2:   Neither is he awed by him.

ACTRESS 1:   A wise soldier is humble.

ACTRESS 3:   Fools win wars, not wise men.

ACTRESS 2:   Victory comes with reason and tactics.

ACTOR 2:   Victory comes with courage.

ACTRESS 1:   Courage is blind, said the wise man.

ACTOR 2:   War is blind, said the fool.

ACTRESS 2:   War makes men noble.

ACTRESS 1:   War degrades life.

ACTRESS 2:   Life is an illusion, said the wise man.

ACTOR 2:   Give me more illusions, said the fool.

ACTRESS 1:   Life is sorrow, said the wise man.

ACTOR 2:   Give me more sorrows, said the fool.

ACTOR 1:   Victory is no sorrow or illusion. To victory!

ACTOR 2:   To victory and to the new Rana soon to see the sun!

ACTRESS 1:   Oh Jai!

     (*Dance of the sacred cow.*)

ACTRESS 2:   The Rani is soon to give birth.

ACTOR 1:   Call a feast of thousand brahmins. Let us celebrate!

ACTRESS 2:   Rani informs her cousin before her husband. Is the Rani giving us an heir?

ACTRESS 1:   Mira is desperate.

ACTRESS 2:   Is she or isn't she?

ACTRESS 1:   I don't know.

ACTRESS 2:   Extraordinary! Either she is or she isn't.

ACTOR 2:   Perhaps we can ask her later.

ACTRESS 2:   No.

ACTOR 1:   Call a feast.

ACTOR 2:   She doesn't seem well.

ACTRESS 2:   We must find out.

ACTOR 1:   Call the brahmins.

ACTOR 2:   She seems sick. Let's wait till later.

ACTOR 1:   Ring the bells!

ACTRESS 1:   Stop! There is no son. There is no son.
There is no son. No. No. Never.

ACTOR 1:   What is happening?

ACTRESS 2:   To be good takes a hundred years; to be bad takes only a day.

ACTOR 2:   I made it up. She didn't say anything.

ACTRESS 1:   I feel like a monkey with a snake in its paw.

ACTOR 1:   Always the beautiful bird is caught.

ACTRESS 2:   To be good, you have to climb up, to be bad you have to climb down.

ACTOR 2:   She wants to give the Rana a son.
She wants to very much. So she believes . . .

ACTRESS 2:   Very strange!

ACTOR 1:   Why did she do it?

ACTRESS 2:   To bring dishonour on Kali.

ACTOR 1:   Prince Jai said it is not her fault.

ACTRESS 2:   Prince Jaimal worries me. Why has he come?

ACTOR 1:   He is a brave fighter. Is Uda jealous?

# 9. No more a Lovers' Quarrel

ACTRESS 1:   Soft music to suggest it's no longer a lovers' quarrel. Rana! O Rana!

ACTOR 1:   Yes.

ACTRESS 1:   You are still here? I mean you haven't gone up . . . I mean I came . . . I came to apologize. It was wrong of me to . . .

ACTOR 1:   Don't talk about it.

ACTRESS 1:   I make so much trouble for the Rana.

ACTOR 1:   I am tired.

ACTRESS 1:   Don't go. I want to talk.

ACTOR 1:   It's late. Go to sleep.

ACTRESS 1:   Can I get you anything?

ACTOR 1:   No.

ACTRESS 1:   Rana . . .

ACTOR 1:   Tomorrow.

ACTRESS 1:   Can I come upstairs?

ACTOR 1:   No.

ACTRESS 1:   But I'm your wife. What's wrong? I want to know.

ACTOR 1:   The Rana strikes her.

ACTRESS 1:   Do it again.

ACTOR 1:   He does.

ACTRESS 1:   Tell me what I should do.

ACTOR 1:   Go away.

   (*And he shuts his door on her face.*)

ACTRESS 1:   Mira looking very hurt, goes and picks up Krishna. She then sprawls on the floor against the same door. She wants to cry but she can't. She brings up her knees, crosses her arms on them, and puts her face on her arms.

   (*Musical transition to hear passage of the night. Dawn music.*)

# 10. I Live in a Golden Cage

❦

ACTRESS 1:   I must have gone to sleep with you in my arm. What a strange dream I had! There I was in a field and I had a baby in my arms. He had shining black eyes, and a black dress and a black turban.

(*Song of the Black Boy.*)

ACTRESS 1:   Mira passes her hand over her belly and takes a deep breath. She looks out at the stars and the mist; she smells the morning, the trees and the grass, then lifts her arms in a sigh.

ACTRESS 3:   Mira? what are you doing at this hour? And look at you with your legs sprawled out like a peasant and your feet facing god.

ACTRESS 1:   Mira self-consciously changes the direction of her feet—away from Kali's image. Then changes direction again. And again. And again until she has made a full unlady-like turn. Oh Jhali, I can't help it. I can't put my feet anywhere because he is everywhere.

ACTRESS 3:   I woke up with a start because I heard the wolves howling. It was black as night. I lit the lamp and went to your room to see if you were safe and asleep. You weren't there! The bed was smooth and cold and empty.

ACTRESS 1:   I live in a golden cage hung with silk; my food is honey and my drink is milk—but all I want is a nest in a tree.

ACTRESS 3:   Where has the Rani been all night?

ACTRESS 1:   Look at the day. How ecstatic it is! Smell the trees and the grass. And the mist and the wind in the sky . . .

ACTRESS 3:   There is no morning without a sun.

ACTRESS 1:   Nor a night without a moon.

ACTRESS 3:   You have been to see someone, haven't you?

ACTRESS 1:   Yes.

ACTRESS 3:   A man?

ACTRESS 1:   Yes.

ACTRESS 3:   Mother, she has a man! A Rani of this house—after all I have done to keep her pure. What if anyone finds out? She also wants to make a liar out of me. I'm an honest woman.

ACTRESS 1:   You can tell the truth.

ACTRESS 3:   If I tell the truth I will be turned out of the house along with you.

ACTRESS 1:   Then do what you like.

ACTRESS 3:   Do what I like? But I am your servant. Oh no! I feel like crying. If the Rana finds out . . .

ACTRESS 1:   He knows.

ACTRESS 3:   Mother—help me! How did he find out?

ACTRESS 1:   He is the one I came to see.

ACTRESS 3:   He is 'the man.' You didn't go to meet another man?

ACTRESS 1:   No.

ACTRESS 3:   Of merciful Mother! You mean everything is all right? What is the meaning of this? What have you been doing here? And with that doll?

ACTRESS 1:   He is not a doll. I fell asleep here. The Rana didn't want me. I tried to go up with him but he shut the door on my face.

ACTRESS 3:   Oh no!

ACTRESS 1:   He doesn't want me anymore.

ACTRESS 3:   No, Mira.

ACTRESS 1:   Love is like a creeper, Jhali; it withers and dies if it has nothing to embrace.

ACTRESS 3:   The Rana didn't call for you, did he?

ACTRESS 1:   He will never call for me now.

ACTRESS 3:   If you are a proper queen the Rana will call for you.

ACTRESS 1:   I am sitting on the shoulder of a man who is sinking in quicksand.

ACTRESS 3:   If you didn't go running after him all the time. You wander all over the palace and the streets after him. You're trembling.

ACTRESS 1:   Will he call me again?

ACTRESS 3:   Do you have fever? I'll get a blanket.

ACTRESS 1:   I think of my son sometimes, and I get afraid.

ACTRESS 3:   Let's go in—I'll make you something hot.

# 11. I'll go Riding in the Forest

❀

(*Dance of the white horse.*)

ACTRESS 1: Do my hair right. I am feeling hot. Here, take the comb. Feel how smooth my hair is. See how it falls on my shoulders. How it reaches down to my hips.

ACTRESS 3: The walls have ears.

ACTRESS 1: My long black hair on my round white hips.

ACTRESS 3: Mira, we will do your hair later. We will bathe you in milk and dip your hair in curds.

ACTRESS 2: There is evil in the air.

ACTOR 1: Is Uda looking after our guest?

ACTRESS 2: Prince Jai is only interested in his cousin. Evil entered our house when she didn't bow to Kali.

ACTOR 1: You can't make a horse by chopping a donkey's ears.

ACTRESS 2: Doesn't the Rana care if his wife is barren?

ACTOR 1: Barren?

ACTRESS 2: That's what they say.

ACTOR 1: Who says?

ACTRESS 2: She's been here a long time and people are talking. Of course I am not saying anything. Barren women are always strange.

ACTOR 1: She has been strange.

ACTRESS 1: Jhali, make me beautiful. Let my hair flow down like a stream—and I shall go riding in the woods with Rana and Jai.

ACTOR 2: Yes. I'll take you for a ride in the forest.

ACTRESS 1: We'll go flying among the trees and the animals; we'll climb hills and descend into cool streams with white horses ahead of us, black ones behind and my hair flying in the clouds. We'll ride fast in the winds and the cold water of the streams will be nectar to my lips.

ACTOR 2: She looks so frail.

ACTRESS 3: No herb will cure love. She never eats anymore since the Rana stopped calling her.

ACTOR 2: He hasn't called for a month.

ACTRESS 3: They've spread a rumour that she's barren. All day she tells me she has let the Rana down.

ACTOR 2:    My cousin was born in the wrong place at the wrong time.

ACTRESS 1:    My head is uncovered. Let me cover my face and my shame.

ACTOR 2:    She is trembling.

ACTRESS 1:    Jai, I am afraid. Let me hold your dry, clean hand. My hand
is wet and dirty. My heart is ahead of me again. It pains so much.

ACTOR 2:    My heart is heavy and I can't bear to see you like this.

ACTRESS 1:    I feel safe with you. Don't go away. I am going to close my
eyes.

ACTOR 2:    Come back to Medta. I shall take care of you. Keep you safe in
my arms, away from everyone. I have missed you very much. Since
you left Medta, I have been wasting away in the desert. Let's go away—
tonight. We will ride through the forest, and no one will know. If they
follow us, we can hide. I'll take care of you . . . keep your warm.

(*Clapping dance.*)

ACTRESS 1:    Jai, O Jai!

ACTOR 2:    Mira, come!

ACTRESS 1:    Jai, O Jai!

# 12. Can you give me a Son

ACTRESS 1: What are you doing? This is my home. Take your hand away from my body. Don't touch me again.

ACTOR 2: Oh, Mira.

ACTRESS 1: Get out!

ACTOR 2: Jai leaves.

ACTRESS 1: Krishna says go; Kali says come.

Krishna, you are all I have left now. Even Jai is gone. I have nowhere to go. What shall I do? I think I'm going to cry. No, I must be brave. Krishna, I never asked you for anything. Can you do something for me? Can you give me a son? I know it's asking a lot. But what are friends for—especially if they are gods. O please, my dear god . . .

(*The dance of Krishna.*)

(*Song of Krishna.*)

# 13. Don't throw Stones at a Broken Tree

ACTRESS 2:    Better to sink in the sea than among men.

ACTOR 1:    Our sister is still young. She should play and be gay.

ACTRESS 2:    A snake's poison and a wasp's sting are better than an unfaithful wife.

ACTOR 2:    Unfaithful wife?

ACTRESS 2:    All day she dances. All night she dances.
And she sings these vulgar songs. She must have someone inside.

ACTOR 1:    Is it the Prince? Oh Mother, she is going mad . . .

ACTRESS 2:    This is known to happen to barren women.
They become possessed of evil spirits.

ACTOR 1:    I have one foot on land and another in water.

ACTRESS 2:    Crows are black all over the world. This is Kali's revenge.

ACTOR 1:    We must move her to another palace. O my glorious ancestors!

ACTRESS 2:    The Neem tree will not become sweet even if you water it with milk.

ACTOR 1:    Don't harm her.

ACTRESS 2:    The snake stings the one who helps him out of the fire.

ACTOR 1:    Don't throw stones at a broken tree.
*(And he leaves.)*

ACTRESS 2:    A stain can be washed, only death removes evil. The witch must die.

# 14. The Cup of Poison

ACTRESS 1:   Make him come to me. I remember it was dark. No one saw us. We went to a thicket and I was so shy. O, he was flattering. My couch was of leaves but his bed was my bosom. His lips were like nectar to mine. And I was drunk in his embrace. He held me tight, I could hardly breathe. After we were together, I felt sweated and moist, hidden away. I thrilled him so. His half closed eyes became restless and he desired me again.

ACTRESS 3:   You can't hide love: when one eye meets another eye it somehow slips out.

ACTRESS 1:   Why doesn't he come to me?

ACTRESS 3:   Let us talk to Krishna—maybe he will help . . .

ACTRESS 1:   Don't mention his name!

ACTRESS 3:   You couldn't be mad if you can scream like that.

ACTRESS 1:   Leave me to my sins.

ACTRESS 3:   Sins! Did I hear correctly?

ACTRESS 1:   Jhali, what does it mean to be attached?

ACTRESS 3:   It is the sweetest and the most painful thing.

ACTRESS 1:   I have the pain and none of the sweetness.

ACTRESS 3:   Who are you attached to?

ACTRESS 1:   Krishna.

ACTRESS 3:   Oh, is that all?

ACTRESS 1:   I want him in a different way.

ACTRESS 3:   I don't understand you. You mean, you mean . . .

ACTRESS 1:   Yes, Yes.

ACTRESS 3:   You mean you lust for him?

ACTRESS 1:   Yes.

ACTRESS 3:   While I was driving a tiger from the front, I find a wolf has entered from the back.

ACTRESS 1:   Listen, I will tell you. When I first discovered this, I looked for the best way to endure it. I tried to hide it, I couldn't. I tried to control it, I couldn't. I finally decided it was best for me to die.

ACTRESS 3:   Die?

ACTRESS 1:   The sky is high but a woman's heart leaps higher.

ACTRESS 3:   Are you mad?

ACTRESS 1:   I am going mad with passion.

ACTRESS 3:   Sugar killed the ant; passion killed the woman. (*Pause.*) How can you feel that way about a god? What arrogance!

ACTRESS 1:   I feel as humble as the earth who kisses the feet of peasants and kings. (*Pause.*) You are hurting me.

ACTRESS 3:   Keep quiet. A person of few words at least escapes slander.

ACTRESS 1:   Stop, you are smothering me.

ACTRESS 3:   Please don't go mad!

ACTRESS 1:   I am not going mad, stupid woman.

ACTRESS 3:   Then look at the world clearly.

ACTRESS 1:   To be clear-sighted is to see yourself.

ACTRESS 3:   What do I see?

ACTRESS 1:   Alive, you don't see your soul. Dead, you don't see your corpse. My soul is the universe. The universe is my lord, Krishna. I am he who I love and he who I love is I.

ACTRESS 3:   Then where is your sin?

ACTRESS 1:   I crave him as a woman and that's sinful. I want him as a woman.

ACTRESS 2:   Enter Uda with a cup.

   (*Dance of the cup.*)

ACTRESS 2:   The Rana has sent this medicine for Mira.

ACTRESS 3:   What is it?

ACTRESS 1:   My dear sister has brought me poison to drink.

ACTRESS 2:   It is medicine for the sick.

ACTRESS 1:   If my husband thinks I am sick, then I am.

   Mira takes it from her.

ACTRESS 3:   Don't drink it.

ACTRESS 1:   I forgive my sister.

ACTRESS 2:   Uda is forgiven by Mira.

ACTRESS 1:   Mira drinks it and finds it nectar.

   (*Song of the Cup.*)

Rana sent a cup of poison,
Mira drank it and laughed.
Bells on her flying feet,
Mira drank it and danced away.

# 15. Since When is She Mirabai

ACTOR 1:   Three months later.

ACTOR 2:   Sounds of an army in retreat. Jai and Rana are on camelback in the hot desert noon of Rajasthan, returning from the war with the Mughal. The up-and-down rhythm of the camel sets the tempo of the scene. The mood is philosophical.

(*Dance of the camels.*)

ACTOR 1:   It is all over my friend, and I feel sad.

ACTOR 2:   Only a battle is lost—not the war.

ACTOR 1:   Fallow ground can be useful; even dead wood is of some use; but a king who has lost a battle is of no use at all. I have fooled myself long enough. If only I had not turned back at least I could have died honourably.

ACTOR 2:   The Rana doesn't do honour to the Sisodia blood.

ACTOR 1:   You can't carve rotten wood. We have lost all our men. Don't speak empty words, Jai. (*Pause.*)

Would you believe it if I told you that the only thing I want now is . . . Mira.

ACTOR 2:   Mira?

ACTOR 1:   I want to go back to her. I miss her.

(*Dance of the creation.*)

ACTOR 2:   (*Chanting.*) Listen:—Brahma took a cluster of bees, gaiety of sunbeams, weeping of clouds, fickleness of wind, timidity of the hare, vanity of the peacock, hardness of stone, sweetness of honey, cruelty of the tiger, the warm glow of fire, coldness of snow, chattering of jays, cooing of the *kokila*, hypocrisy of the crane, and the fidelity of the rainbird—he put all of these together, made her into a woman, and gave her to man. Eight days later man returned the woman to Brahma lamenting:—'She chatters all the time, cries for no reason, and is always ill. Take her back.' Brahma took her back.

Eight days again passed, and man returned to Brahma with a sigh:—'Since she left there is no one to sing and dance with me, play with me, glance at me, and cling to me. Give her back.' And Brahma returned her to man.

Three days later, man returned crying, 'I can't live with her.'

The story has no ending.

ACTRESS 3:    Many years ago, when Mira was a little girl, she saw marriage procession. She went in and told her grandmother that she too wanted a bridegroom. Her grandmother jokingly took Mira to Krishna's shrine, pointed to him and said, 'This is your bridegroom.' Since that day she has been very attached to it.

ACTOR 1:    Noble Jai, it's time you married. What about the Princess Uda? We would be honoured to have you as our brother-in-law.

ACTOR 2:    I am already that.

ACTOR 1:    We are thirsty.

ACTOR 2:    I shall get some water.

ACTOR 1:    When drinking water remember the source.

ACTRESS 1:    (*Chanting.*) On top of the highest heaven, above the dwelling place of the gods, by the dark and gentle river lives Krishna, the eternal lover.

The sunshine on the riverbank blues his slender shoulders as he joyously bathes to the sound of the Name, the sound current.

In the dusk of the day an eon long, beside the blue-flowered meadow where cattle graze, peacocks dance and nightingales sing, the blue-lover plays his flute.

Women of the world and goddesses of the heavens hear his call and leave their homes and husbands, and honour go to him. And they love him.

The blue-god, ever young, laughs and plays and wrestles with them in the shade of the scented sallow wood tree, and fulfills their yearning hearts—every single one of them.

Krishna the beautiful, the radiant, the graceful, the exciting, is giving and receiving joy.

ACTOR 1:    Here we are! Where is the Rani? Doesn't the Rani come to greet the Rana?

ACTRESS 2:    Prepare the fire for the holy anointment!

ACTOR 1:    The Rana has lost, and there will be no fires.

ACTRESS 2:    The Rana has won the biggest victory.

ACTOR 1:    It is all over, and I am tired.

ACTRESS 2:    Mirabai is the Rana's victory.

ACTOR 1:    It is all over, and I want the Rani.

ACTRESS 2:    The Rana cannot touch Mirabai.

ACTOR 1:     Since when, is she Mirabai?

ACTOR 2:     What has happened to her?

ACTOR 1:     What is wrong with our sister?

ACTRESS 2:   I gave her a cup . . .

ACTOR 1:     Is there another man?

ACTRESS 3:   She is the purest queen in the world.

ACTRESS 2:   To preserve the honour of the family, forgive me, O Krishna, I gave her a cup of poison.

ACTOR 1:     The Rana slaps his sister.

ACTRESS 2:   She drank from the cup, and it was nectar to her lips. She sang and we knew.

ACTOR 1:     Mira has gone mad.

ACTRESS 3:   That is not all. Two days ago, she was in the garden picking flowers. I was with her. In her flower basket I saw a snake. I screamed with terror and asked her to run inside . . .

ACTRESS 2:   I heard the scream and came out. She was playing with the snake.

ACTRESS 3:   She was singing to a deadly poisonous cobra.

ACTOR 1:     Jhali has also gone mad.

ACTRESS 2:   She has changed us all.

ACTOR 1:     Women without men become mad.

ACTRESS 3:   She is a saint!

ACTOR 1:     She is my wife.

ACTRESS 1:   (*Song Celestial.*) There is true knowledge,
                            Knew it is this:
                            To see one changeless life in all the lives,
                            And in the separate, one inseparable!

ACTOR 1:     Does the whole kingdom know that my wife is mad? The peasants want any excuse to swallow miracles. But my sister should know better.

ACTRESS 2:   Dear brother, she has raised Mewar to its highest.

ACTOR 1:     I have lost the war; I have lost my wife.

# 16. Why should I be Angry?

ACTRESS 1:   Enter Mira looking detached, serene and beautiful in white.
(*Procession of the idol.*)

ACTOR 1:   Mira!

ACTRESS 1:   Yes, Rana.

ACTOR 1:   Are you well?

ACTRESS 1:   Yes.

ACTOR 1:   Why didn't you come to greet me when I arrived?

ACTRESS 1:   I was praying.

ACTOR 1:   Did I disturb you?

ACTRESS 1:   No.

ACTOR 1:   Rana trying to keep the conversation going.
We have come home.

ACTRESS 1:   Yes, I know.

ACTOR 1:   Aren't you happy that we have returned?

ACTRESS 1:   Yes.

ACTOR 1:   I failed.

ACTRESS 1:   No.

ACTOR 1:   Come here and sit down.

ACTRESS 1:   She sits down beside him.

ACTOR 1:   He takes her hand and tries to sound enthusiastic.
I missed you.

ACTRESS 1:   Did you?

ACTOR 1:   Why is your hand so cold?

ACTRESS 1:   Is it?

ACTOR 1:   Are you angry with me?

ACTRESS 1:   Why should I be angry?

ACTOR 1:   Rana trying to make a joke, but actually deadly serious.
*I* should be angry. You have been playing with snakes and drinking cups of poison, and making a fool of yourself.

ACTRESS 1:   When wine finishes you turn elsewhere; when youth finishes you turn inside.

ACTOR 1:   You are going!

ACTRESS 1:   The real treasure is inside me.

ACTOR 1:    Come upstairs to sleep with me.

ACTRESS 1:    I have to wait for Krishna.

ACTOR 1:    Where is he?

ACTRESS 1:    He is inside me. Just as the seed is in the tree and the tree is inside the seed; so I am in him and he is inside me.

ACTOR 1:    Come later.

ACTRESS 1:    Krishna stays with me the whole night.

ACTOR 1:    I'll lie down here.

(*And he lies down.*)

ACTRESS 1:    Mira begin to fan him.

ACTOR 1:    You too, lie down.

ACTRESS 1:    I am not sleepy.

(*He feigns sleeping for his own pride's sake. She continues to fan him. She gets up, blows out the lamp and is about to leave when the Rana tries to embrace her forcibly.*)

Don't touch me.

ACTOR 1:    You are my wife.

# 17. Don't ask the Blindman the Way

꧁꧂

ACTRESS 2:   Does the Rana know that we are leaving?

ACTOR 2:   Yes.

ACTRESS 2:   Did he say anything?

ACTOR 2:   Nothing.

ACTRESS 2:   What did you tell him?

ACTOR 2:   I told him that . . . that Mirabai and Uda were going off to the Vrindavan forest.

ACTRESS 2:   Did he believe you?

ACTOR 2:   He knows he has lost you both forever.

ACTRESS 2:   How is he?

ACTOR 2:   Lonely.

ACTRESS 2:   Oh Jai!

ACTOR 2:   He is having a temple built for Mira. He forgets she is going away forever.

ACTRESS 2:   Jai, why don't you stay on a while, and look after him.

ACTOR 2:   This is his wife's duty.
   *(Pause.)*
   I have to live my own life. (*Passionately*).
   If you *wise* and *saintly* people have given up living, why should I?

ACTRESS 2:   Rana appears in the grey light of the door. He has a tragic radiance.

ACTOR 1:   Jai, I think we need more colour in Mira's temple.
   I feel fresh after a cold bath in this hot weather. Let's have a drink to cold baths!
   I remember the day she arrived. She brought youth, love—so much of it. She used to go to the garden to pick flowers early in the morning. She used to follow me like a shadow, wherever I went, afraid we would be separated. She wouldn't eat until she had fed me by her hand . . .
   *(The Rana repairs the tank after it is empty.)*

ACTOR 2:   Time doesn't turn back.

ACTOR 1:   Ask them to stop those bells! If the people want to follow Mira's god let them do it quietly.

ACTOR 2:    Those are Kali's bells, Rana.

ACTOR 1:    Kali is leaving us. If Kali wants to leave, let her leave quietly. This house is doomed. There will be no more Ranas, no more victories, no more Kali, no more Mewar. It is over!

ACTOR 2:    The house of Mewar must live forever.

ACTOR 1:    When you're not going to live a hundred, why plan for a thousand.

You are going too, Jai?

ACTOR 2:    Yes, Rana.

ACTOR 1:    It is going to be quiet here with everyone gone. I can smell the emptiness. I am going to spend the rest of my days amusing myself by counting the spider webs growing from floors to the ceiling. Old age comes slowly, especially if you have to wait for it.

# 18. I'm Blinded

ACTRESS 1: Shh . . . my friends. Silence! I hear the flute. He has come. Oh look, he smiles at me. The time has come. I have waited all my life for this moment. The time for the play is over and I must leave. I am a bride today and I'm going to his home of infinite happiness. He is calling now.

Dance, my heart! Joy! Mira is in the arms of her beloved.

Listen to His melody. O world, hear His divine Name—the glory of His Word. And see how the hills, the sea and the earth sway to the rhythm of His sound current.

(*Mira's Song.*)

Mira's heart feels so light. I am free—free from life and death and time. Look at his light, shining like a thousand, thousand suns. My eyes shrink from his splendour, brilliant like fire, blazing, boundless. Ah, it ravishes me! O light of lights! He outshines the brightest moon and star. I am blinded. But how I love my blindness. I'm blinded.

(*Fade*)

# 9 Jakhoo Hill

The first performance of the play took place on 6 June 1996 at Kamani Auditorium, New Delhi, with the following cast:

| | |
|---|---|
| Karan Chand (Mamu) | Bhaskar Ghose |
| Chitra | Sinia Jain |
| Deepak | Rupin Jayal |
| Amrita | Kusum Haidar |
| P.N. Rai (Rai Saheb) | Ajay Balram |
| Ansuya | Shyama Haldar |

*The production was designed by Anjolie Ela Menon and*
*Produced by Joy Michael/Ajay Balram*
*Directed by Sunit Tandon*

# Characters

*[In order of appearance]*

MAMU (KARAN CHAND)

CHITRA

DEEPAK

AMRITA

RAI SAHEB

ANSUYA

*The action of the play takes place over two days around Diwali in 1962 in an upper middle class house at Jakhoo Hill in Simla. The play is in four acts, divided by an interval during Act 3 when Ansuya and Deepak leave for her room*

# Act One

[Opens on Karan.]

KARAN: Thank you for coming this evening to watch the unfolding of the events at 9 Jakhoo Hill, Simla. The play is set in 1962. It revolves around two families of Lahore and what happened to them after Independence, or, more correctly, after the Partition—that great tearing apart, which reduced people to elemental, fearful creatures; desperate to survive, clinging to the vestiges of dignity.

Well, these two families survived. One of them consists of a lady from a fine old family, her young daughter and her brother. Her husband died in the riots; they lost all they had in Lahore and came away to Delhi, where they had a couple of mills and a big, sprawling house in the Civil Lines. But she and her brother were no managers and, after their father died a few years later, they were all at sea. As the losses mounted, they had to sell the mills, then their house, and they moved to Simla—to 9 Jakhoo Hill, once their summer residence. This was all they had been left with, and a meagre income from bonds and shares, much too inadequate for their way of life.

The other family is of a young man, a successful executive in Bombay and his mother, who endured the terrors of Partition, and moved to Mumbai, where the mother, with an obsessive devotion, ensured that her son got the best education and then a good job in a good company. She has a husband, but he doesn't count, so you won't see him.

(Enter in a separate area, Chitra and Deepak, carrying luggage. They sit on a bench.)

Here they are, waiting at Kalka station for their connecting train to Simla. This is Deepak, the young man. He's a bright, cheerful young man, eager to get on, and very, very conscious of his mother. His mother, Chitra, is a survivor: street-smart, calculating and unconcerned about her ways. She has one item on her agenda: to push her son up.

(Enter Amrita, in the upstage area, adjusting her sari, examining herself in a mirror, and obviously getting ready to go out for the evening)

The other family now: Amrita, over there, was born into a distinguished family, as I said, into a world of grace, refinement and good taste,
and, of course, great wealth. That world is gone, but she clings to her
memories.

(*Doorbell rings. Amrita goes to the door and receives Rai Saheb, and ush-
ers him to the sofa, chatting and collecting her purse, shawl and umbrella.*)

Gentle and caring, she is trying to cope. She is talking to a family
friend, Mr P.N. Rai, ICS, a Secretary to the Government of India,
who is one of that breed which is more British than the British. As
you will see, he plays a major role in the events that follow.

(*Amrita calls for Ansuya and the latter enters. Amrita tells her she is going
out; she and Rai Saheb leave. Ansuya is left looking out of the French
windows.*)

And that girl there is Ansuya, Amrita's daughter. She was not
born to lead a staid, conventional life. Lonely, withdrawn, but with
an almost fierce vitality, she wants to live fully and passionately.

Finally, there is her uncle, Amrita's brother, Karan Chand. (*Looks
around on stage, sees no other actor. Turns to audience with a sheepish smile*)

Me. I incurred my father's wrath by becoming a teacher and
taught for a while at the University. But the crisis in our family obliged
me to give up my job and, after an hopeless attempt to run the mills,
I gave up . . . well, just gave up, to live with my sister and with Ansuya,
my niece . . . Ansuya, who was the centre of my . . . but we must get
on with the story.

(*Lights fade out on the two areas of Chitra–Deepak and Ansuya.*)

I must take you back now to (*looks at newspaper on the table.*) the
twenty-fourth of October, 1962, just before Diwali. The Chinese have
invaded India and every day the papers are full of sad, humiliating
news of Indian defeats. It is breaking Nehru's heart. The country
hasn't yet realized that it is dangerous to put dreamers in power. It
saddens me, as it does many of us, because we once believed in the
same, hopeless dreams.

This is the living room of our home, 9 Jakhoo Hill. Tatty? Well, it
is: it reflects our condition, but you can see that it was once an elegant
room, like the house itself. The house was about a way of life; the
way we were.

It is nearly midnight. So, let's start the story.

(*Full lights on the drawing room. The furniture, drapes and upholstery—*

*all conspire to convey the impression that the occupants have seen better times. There is a large, old-fashioned radio prominently placed on stage left.*

*It has been a damp October, but the fire at the back makes the room appear cosy. Mamu is sitting near the fireplace on an easy chair, next to a standing lamp. He has a shawl around his shoulders and is engrossed in the final moves of a chess game. He is forty-eight years old.*

*There is another chair directly opposite him, which is empty. It is late, almost midnight. The bells of Jakhoo Temple can be heard in the distance.*

*Ansuya enters with a cup of tea. She is twenty-six, intelligent but impulsive. She wears a comfortable salwar-kameez.)*

ANSUYA:   Here is some tea, Mamu. It will warm you.

MAMU:   (*Without looking up.*) Knight to queen six. It's a mate. I'm afraid . . . um . . . you can't move anywhere. (*Taking the tea.*)

ANSUYA:   But you always win. (*She goes up to him affectionately, puts her arm around his neck. She sneezes.*)

Mamu, you must do something about your cat. It drank the milk again today. I had to make tea with powdered milk.

MAMU:   (*Drinking the tea.*) It tastes all right.

ANSUYA:   But we can't have the cat drink our milk every day.

MAMU:   It's late, and your mother still hasn't come back.

ANSUYA:   Is that surprising? Dinner rarely gets to the table before eleven at the Rai Saheb's, even on a normal day. (*Frowning.*)

Besides, Amma will be desperately trying to recapture her past.

MAMU:   The past always looks better because it isn't here. Why didn't you . . . er . . . go to the party?

ANSUYA:   (*Wearily.*) You know the types at Rai Saheb's parties—you can always predict what they are going to say. There's a war on, but they'll be laughing drinking and talking about everything else except what matters. Simla contains two types of people—those who are bored and those who are bores.

MAMU:   (*Laughs.*) But you never go out, Ansu.

ANSUYA:   I hate parties, Mamu. I feel as if I'm on display like a sari at Leela Ram's shop. I can tell by their looks. (*And she mimicks.*)

'Such a nice girl, Ansuya Malik—I wonder why she hasn't got married?' It is humiliating, Mamu.

MAMU:   (*Hesitantly.*) Shall we . . . um . . . have another game?

ANSUYA:   (*Petulantly.*) No, no. I'm tired of playing.

MAMU:   (*Hurt.*) With me?

ANSUYA:   Look at us. It's the night before Diwali and here we are, killing time, playing chess. Of course, there's no question of celebrating this year, but it's not just the war. Mamu, do you remember the excitement at Diwali when Papa was alive? The servants bumping into each other, beating carpets, scrubbing the floors, cleaning the drapes—everyone was in a hurry and the house was full of confusion. There'd be new clothes for everyone. And comings and goings and puja. I used to be so excited. I could hardly sleep. What has happened to us, Mamu?

MAMU:   Well, for one thing, we don't have the money.

ANSUYA:   And why don't we have the money?

MAMU:   You're not going to start on your mother again.

ANSUYA:   Yesterday, she gave Bhola a thousand rupees to get married, when the others haven't been paid for months.

MAMU:   She is generous, Ansu.

ANSUYA:   But someone has to run the house. (*Suddenly her eyes are filled with tears.*)

And now, even this house will have to be sold.

MAMU:   Shh!

ANSUYA:   (*Getting angry.*) Who are we trying to fool!

MAMU:   Shh! The walls have ears.

ANSUYA:   Thank God! Amma was in the bath this morning when the broker came.

MAMU:   (*Afraid.*) What happened?

ANSUYA:   I had to turn him away.

MAMU:   Oh no!

ANSUYA:   Yes, everyone knows.

MAMU:   How humiliating!

ANSUYA:   (*In tears.*) Everyone knows that the house is going to be sold, except the owners.

MAMU:   (*Consoling her.*) Now, now, Ansu, don't be upset.

ANSUYA:   That is Simla for you! The whole town knows everything in twenty-four hours if it is raining, and in twelve hours if it is not.
(*Pause.*)

Mamu, I want to go away. Away from this drab life. All we ever do is talk and talk. And we eat, and we sleep, get up in the morning and do the same again. I want to *do* something.

MAMU:    Are you tired of me?

ANSUYA:    I'm tired of the life we lead.

MAMU:    I thought maybe . . . maybe I had said something that offended you.

ANSUYA:    You always twist everything.

MAMU:    Well, it is just you and me here. So I thought . . .

ANSUYA:    It's got nothing to do with you. Don't be so touchy, Mamu. I want to get out. I am getting old.

MAMU:    I'm the one who is old, and of no use to anyone. Look at me. Don't I look old?

ANSUYA:    No.

MAMU:    Doesn't this . . . grey and this bald patch suggest that I am old? Don't I sort of fade into the background, like old furniture?

ANSUYA:    No, you look fine.

MAMU:    (*Eagerly.*) Do I?

ANSUYA:    Yes.

MAMU:    (*Eagerly.*) Really? Tell me that I'm still young.

ANSUYA:    (*Impatiently.*) Yes.
(*Pause.*) Shall I tell you what I really want? (*He nods.*)
You'll laugh at me.

MAMU:    Tell me.
(*She goes and takes a book from the fireplace.*)

ANSUYA:    (*Whispering.*) I want to go far, far away, to a place where no one knows me. I want to work . . . and . . . work where everyone is busy and no one asks questions.
(*Pause.*)
Mamu, there's something bursting out of me . . .

MAMU:    What's that book?

ANSUYA:    This? Oh, it is a guidebook. On Bombay. Deepak sent it to me.

MAMU:    (*His eyes widening.*) You want to go and work in *Bombay*!
(*She nods.*)

MAMU:    Deepak, Deepak! All you do is talk about Deepak.

ANSUYA:    (*Defiantly.*) So what?

MAMU:    I . . . I don't like him.

ANSUYA:    Why?

MAMU:    I don't know . . . he's selfish . . . and I'm afraid you'll get hurt.
(*Pause.*)

ANSUYA:    Well, he's coming tomorrow.

MAMU: I know he's coming tomorrow. Why is he coming tomorrow?

ANSUYA: Because Amma invited them and…and I want him to come. (*Defiantly.*)
So?

MAMU: Now, look here, Ansuya.

ANSUYA: Yes, Mamu?

MAMU: (*Checks.*) You're grown up now. Do you have to keep calling me 'Mamu?'

ANSUYA: But you are my Mamu.

MAMU: Nothing. Just that when we talk, I completely lose myself in our world. Then you say 'Mamu,' and I suddenly wake up and there's a gap.

ANSUYA: A gap?

MAMU: I begin to feel old and responsible and your uncle. It was different when you were little, and you held my finger when we went for a walk.

ANSUYA: All right. I'll try, Mamu.

MAMU: There you go again . . .

ANSUYA: (*Laughs.*) Oops! But what am I to call you?

MAMU: Call me by my name. Call me 'Karan.'

ANSUYA: (*Self-consciously.*) All right, I'll try, K . . . Kar . . . (*she cannot say it.*) Mamu, I can't help it. When I see you, 'Mamu' comes out.

MAMU: I see. So I'm nothing more than a 'Mamu' to you?
        (*She looks embarrassed. He tries to hide his own embarrassment.*)

ANSUYA: Dear Mamu, you *are* fond of me.

MAMU: More than my life.

ANSUYA: (*Laughing.*) You're so dramatic.
(*Sound of footsteps.*)
(*Vivaciously.*) Oh, she's come! She's come!
(*She opens the door.*)
Amma, is that you?
(*She stops herself as she sees Rai Saheb ahead of Amrita. Rai Saheb— 'Bunty' to his friends—man of the world, handsome, and a successful member of the Indian Civil Service (the ICS). He is in his mid-fifties (but could pass for a younger man), sports an ascot, a tweed jacket, and a pipe. The sort of person who speaks Hindustani with an Oxford accent. He has a distinguished look, helped in part by his silver grey hair at the temples. Amrita, Ansuya's mother, is a year older than her brother, Karan. She wears an elegant silk sari.*)

RAI SAHEB:   Ansu, I say, you owe me ten chips.

ANSUYA:   Oh, hello, Bunty Uncle! Why do I owe you ten chips?

RAI SAHEB:   Because Dinky finally ditched Sushma.

ANSUYA:   No! Poor Sushma!

AMRITA:   And they were so much in love!

ANSUYA:   Indian boys are spineless.

RAI SAHEB:   (*Gloating.*) As I predicted . . . Dinky's mother did not approve.

AMRITA:   And they made such a lovely pair.

ANSUYA:   But didn't Dinky put up a fight?

RAI SAHEB:   Worse, Dinky's got engaged to some rich '*bhenji*' from Amritsar.

ANSUYA:   Someone he's never met?

MAMU:   It's the old story. Boy meets girl. Boy conquers girl. Boy abandons girl.

   (*Pause.*)

RAI SAHEB:   Which reminds me have you heard? Our troops have abandoned Tawang. Biji Kaul is lying sick in bed in Delhi and the Chinese are just going to walk right in. I told them in Delhi that this would happen; but, of course, Mr Krishna Menon has to have his own way.

ANSUYA:   It's all so frightening.

AMRITA:   The wind is blowing again.

ANSUYA:   (*Goes to the window.*) It looks like it's going to rain.

AMRITA:   Simla will be nicely washed and cleaned for Chitra and Deepak tomorrow.

ANSUYA:   Amma, I'm so excited that Deepak is coming. We're going to have Diwali after all.

MAMU:   We don't need Deepaks to have a Diwali.

ANSUYA:   Mamu!

AMRITA:   Why don't you come over tomorrow evening, Bunty, and meet our guests?

RAI SAHEB:   If there is good whiskey and pretty women, I never say no.

AMRITA:   Good!

   (*To Ansuya, enthusiastically.*)

   Ansu, Rai Saheb is taking the young people to a picnic on Friday. Of course you'll go?

ANSUYA:   No.

AMRITA:   I know—you can take Deepak with you.

RAI SAHEB:    There will be Dinky and Nina, and Bubbly and Flukey and . . . I say, do you know that the Khannas' ayah is pregnant?

ANSUYA:    (*Fascinated.*) What? Who is the father?

RAI SAHEB:    (*Smiling.*) Naughty, naughty! When I mentioned it to Colonel Khanna this evening, he, of course, went red.

> (*He laughs.*)

And if the Colonel hadn't been in his best third peg, bum bum ho ho mood...

AMRITA:    Shame on you, Bunty, gossiping like this.

RAI SAHEB:    (*To Ansuya.*) Well, my dear?

ANSUYA:    What?

RAI SAHEB:    The picnic.

> (*Clearing his throat.*)

I'll manage the Governor's Rest House, in case it rains.

> (*Uncomfortable pause.*)

ANSUYA:    No, thank you, Bunty Uncle.

RAI SAHEB:    I say, come to think of it, one rarely sees you on the Mall these days.

ANSUYA:    (*Smiling ironically.*) One never sees me on the Mall these days.

RAI SAHEB:    (*Tempo increasing as he speaks.*) But what is there to do in Simla, my dear—except go to the Mall every evening; find your friends eating ice cream at Scandal Point; drag them to the Green Room for the latest gossip; rush to Rivoli for the new picture; plan picnics to Anandale and Mashobra; and throng to the Sunday morning for bingo and beer!

MAMU:    (*With irony.*) A remarkable way to live, don't you think, when our jawans are dying on the front?

RAI SAHEB:    (*As if noticing him for the first time.*) Eh, I say . . . The professor speaks! (*Turning to Amrita.*)

I say, is it true about your house?

AMRITA:    (*Turning pale.*) What about this house?

RAI SAHEB:    (*Realizing his mistake.*) No, nothing.

AMRITA:    (*In a loud, unnatural voice.*) What about this house, Bunty?

RAI SAHEB:    I must be mistaken.

AMRITA:    (*Almost screaming.*) Bunty, what about this house?

RAI SAHEB:    (*Sheepishly.*) Well, that it's up for sale.

AMRITA:    (*In tears.*) Who says it's up for sale? Filthy lies!

RAI SAHEB:    (*Trying to make up.*) You know Simla, my dear. There's nothing else to do but gossip. Why, when I heard it, my reaction was, 'What nonsense!'

AMRITA:     (*Recovering.*) Bunty, have some coffee?

RAI SAHEB:    (*Looking at his watch.*) No, thank you, my dear; must be getting along, if I don't want to get caught in this storm. I say, ta-ta, cheerio. Happy Diwali and all that! (*Exit.*)

ANSUYA:     (*Mimicking him, as she closes the door behind him.*) 'I say, ta-ta, cheerio, Happy Diwali and all that.'

AMRITA:     (*Giving her a disapproving look.*) Ansu!

ANSUYA:     (*Mimicking.*) 'I say, one rarely sees you on the Mall these days.'
          (*Mamu laughs.*)

AMRITA:     Stop it! It's not nice.

ANSUYA:     The conceit of the man, Amma!

AMRITA:     How do you like my new sari?
          (*And she turns around to show it to everyone.*)

MAMU:      It's beautiful!

ANSUYA:     It should be. It's *the* most expensive sari in Simla.

AMRITA:     And how do you know?

ANSUYA:     Because Leela Ram's man delivered it this afternoon.

AMRITA:     And you saw the price?

ANSUYA:     Someone has to think of money, Amma.

AMRITA:     (*Animatedly.*) The Colonel complimented me on it, and Mrs Dewan kept looking at it the whole evening.
          (*To Ansuya.*)
Oh Ansu, it's not right to stay by yourself all evening long, evening after evening. Why don't you go out at least once in a while?

ANSUYA:     No.

AMRITA:     (*Angrily.*) Then you won't get married.

ANSUYA:     I don't care.

AMRITA:     Of course you do.

ANSUYA:     These boys don't want to marry me, Amma.

AMRITA:     How do you know?

ANSUYA:     Because no boy has the guts to marry without a dowry. Look at Dinky. We all thought that he would marry . . .

AMRITA:     (*Defensively.*) I suppose it's my fault that you don't have a dowry?

ANSUYA:     Amma . . .

AMRITA:     If your father hadn't squandered all that money away . . .

ANSUYA:   He did not.
          (*In tears.*)
Why do you keep saying that?

AMRITA:   Your grandfather married off nine daughters like princesses.

ANSUYA:   (*Wearily.*) What's the use, Amma!

AMRITA:   You're stubborn, like your father. Proud and vain . . .

ANSUYA:   Why blame him? Look at yourself.

AMRITA:   (*Cut to the quick.*) What!

ANSUYA:   (*Defensively.*) Well, look at what's happened to the mills ever since
          he died.

AMRITA:   Mind what you say, girl!

ANSUYA:   All we keep doing is selling off our properties.

AMRITA:   We have debts to pay off.
          (*About to break down.*)
You don't understand these things.

ANSUYA:   And now, even this house will be gone.

AMRITA:   No . . . it won't.

ANSUYA:   Everyone seems to know about it except us.

AMRITA:   (*Pointing to the drapes.*) See those drapes, Ansu? Your father
          brought them from England, and they were the talk of the town that
          season. Oh, the parties we used to have, Ansu! The servants were
          forever polishing the silver. Why, the whole of Nehru's first Cabinet
          must have dined here some time or another.

ANSUYA:   It's over, Amma; this house is as good as gone.

AMRITA:   No!
          (*Covering her ears with her hands.*)
I don't want to hear about it.

ANSUYA:   But, Amma, you can't keep running away . . .

AMRITA:   (*In tears.*) Don't say it!

ANSUYA:   Amma, please, you've got to . . .

AMRITA:   (*Beginning to cry.*) Well. I've done my best. What more do you
          want me to do? It's too much. It's not fair!
          (*Ansuya goes and embraces her.*)

ANSUYA:   Oh Amma, don't cry! Please, my darling Amma. Don't cry!
          (*Fade.*)

# Act Two

❧

[*Stage Centre. Spotlight on Karan, the narrator.*]

KARAN: They say you never get a second chance to make a first impression. So, what sort of impression have we made on you? Pretty lot, our family. No one's happy. But then, most families are like that, aren't they? Yes, all families want to be happy, but they live in a way that they can't help but be unhappy.

What is happiness, anyway? You are dropped into the world one fine day, and you are snuffed out another, without so much as a warning. And in between, you try to snatch a few moments of happiness . . . and discover too late that it wasn't happiness after all. And it doesn't matter whether you are at the top or at the bottom of the social scale.

(*Pause.*)

As you can see, our life had a certain rhythm, a certain quality, even as we were slowly getting poorer. It is this rhythm which was shattered when Deepak and Chitra came into our lives.

(*Lights come on gradually. The same room.*)

It is the next morning, around noon. It is bright and fresh, the way Simla feels after a shower. The sun is peering in from the open window. From the window, you can glimpse the Himalayas in the distance; a bit hazy today, but usually you can see the white peaks gleaming in the sun.

(*He takes the newspaper from under his arm.*)

The paper has arrived with more dismal news from the Eastern front. Tawang has just fallen and General Thapar says we are preparing to put up a stand at Se La. And I can smell the blood! 'Fallen,' 'put up a stand' . . . They think they can fool us with their words. Nehru and Krishna Menon are merely living out their illusions of grandeur. Tchhah!

(*Speaking privately, in a hushed tone.*)

Oh! I forgot to introduce a rather important character: she plays a significant role in the events that follow, even if it is behind the scenes. She is Sandhya Rani, Queen of the Night—my cat.

But, let's get on with the story.

*(A song from an early 60s film is playing on the radio. Mamu is sitting near the window, with the paper, tapping his foot to the music. Amrita enters with a cup of tea. She stands looking affectionately at Mamu for a while, seeing that he is lost in the music. After a while, Mamu notices her and turns down the volume with a smile.)*

MAMU:  I . . . er . . . practically fell in love with Waheeda Rehman after seeing that picture. She had such beautiful eyes! *(Hesitates.)* Ansu's eyes . . . er . . . are a bit like hers, don't you think?

*(Amrita frowns. Mamu continues to hum the last bars of the song.)*

We saw it at the Rivoli, remember?

*(Pause.)*

AMRITA:  What time is their train coming?

MAMU:  *(Looking at his watch.)* They should be coming any minute now.

*(Mamu switches off the radio. Pause.)*

Why are they coming?

AMRITA:  What do you mean?

MAMU:  Well, Chitra always has . . . um . . . a reason . . . Has she ever come just to visit? . . . er . . . What does she want this time?

AMRITA:  *(Dismissing him.)* You're impossible. When did Ansuya go to the station?

MAMU:  She must have left . . . er . . . an hour ago.

AMRITA:  *(Worried.)* I hope there's enough milk in the house. Deepak loves his glass of milk at bedtime.

*(Coughs.)*

I wish you would do something about your cat, Karan. She finished the milk again last night. She sheds hair all over the house.

*(Coughs.)*

I'm sure she has given me this cough.

MAMU:  'The trouble with a kitten is that
It eventually becomes a cat.'

AMRITA:  It is unnatural to be so fond of a cat. If you had married, you would have had a wife to look after, instead of a cat.

MAMU:  *(Laughing at himself.)* I am too old to be married.

AMRITA:  *(Severely.)* Whose fault is it that you did not marry when the best matches were available? After a brilliant college career, and then you got into the ICS . . . You could have married any girl, but no, the ways of ordinary people were not good enough for you. The sun shines only once in life, Karan.

MAMU:    Have I changed a lot since then?

AMRITA:    Yes, you have, Karan Chand. You were young and handsome then. Now, you have aged. And you talk all the time, like old people. Of the Partition, of Lahore . . .

MAMU:    These kids will never know what it meant to grow up in Lahore—the poetry, the music, the intellectual discussions . . . Ah, it was heaven to be young in Lahore!

AMRITA:    See what I mean? Karan, you live in the past. And you complain. There's a bitterness in your voice.

MAMU:    Why does Ansuya write so often to Deepak?

AMRITA:    Why? What's wrong with that?

MAMU:    Nothing. It's just that she's become so secretive.

AMRITA:    He is a nice young man, Karan.

MAMU:    It could be serious, you know.

AMRITA:    Hush, they are just good friends.

MAMU:    No.

AMRITA:    How do you know?

MAMU:    I just know, that's all.

(*Sounds outside. Excited voices. Chitra enters, followed by Ansuya and Deepak. Deepak touches Amrita's feet. Amrita and Chitra embrace. Mamu's eyes are fixed on his niece.*

*Deepak, twenty-seven, squarely built, is full of energy and ambition. He is talented and smooth, but he is also under the excessive influence of his mother. Having had to come up the hard way, he has cultivated the social graces, including a public school way of speaking English ('What the hell, yaar,' 'Give him ten chips, yaar.') He is one of those persons who will succeed in the eyes of the world. He has already done well for himself, and knows he is good. He has a composed voice, shining eyes and a bright smile. He is self-possessed and good-natured. One of those persons who looks amiably perplexed at an unpleasant situation, as though he can't understand why anyone should be angry with him.*

*Chitra, his mother, is slightly younger than Amrita. She is attractive in a fleshy and flashy sort of way. Wears synthetic saris, too low to be tasteful. She is coarse, has no qualms about taking advantage of people and will go to any lengths to make sure her son succeeds in life. She speaks with Punjabi mannerisms ('Helloji,' 'Thank youji'.)*

AMRITA:    Ah, here they are, here they are.

CHITRA:    Didi!

DEEPAK:  Happy Diwali, everyone!

CHITRA:  Bhai Saheb, Namaste!

AMRITA:  (*Genuinely happy.*) Come here, my son, let me look at you. How handsome you've become! Why, half the girls in Bombay must be after you.

    (*She puts her arm around him.*)

MAMU:  And their mothers, too.

    (*Deepak sneezes.*)

CHITRA:  Watch it Deepak, you'll catch a cold in this weather. *Banian pai hain na?*

DEEPAK:  (*Glaring at his mother.*) Ma . . .

CHITRA:  He's still my baby.

    (*Sniffing the air.*) I smell a cat.

    (*Deepak sneezes again*).

    My God! Deepak has an allergy to cats.

ANSUYA:  Mamu's cat!

CHITRA:  There *is* a cat!

AMRITA:  Karan, here, has a cat, instead of a wife.

MAMU:  When things go wrong in this house, it's usual to blame the cat. Er . . . mind you, my cat has insomnia.

CHITRA:  Insomnia?

DEEPAK:  It means that it 'can't sleep,' Ma.

CHITRA:  I knew cats got sick, but I never knew one which suffered from not being able to sleep . . . what was that word?

DEEPAK:  'Insomnia,' Ma.

CHITRA:  Didi, how will Deepak sleep, with a non-sleeping cat in the house?

MAMU:  I'll keep the non-sleeper in my room.

CHITRA:  Oh, thank you, Karanji.

AMRITA:  We'll make sure he locks it away for your entire visit.

DEEPAK:  (*Going to the window.*) I say, what a view, yaar!

ANSUYA:  Even though I look at it every day, I don't tire of the Himalayas.

CHITRA:  *Arre Didi, yeh kamra kuchh badla-badla-sa nahin lag raha?*

    (*Looking around.*)

    What's happened? It's so empty.

DEEPAK:  (*Taking a deep breath.*) But the smell is the same. I still remember the wonderful smell of this house.

AMRITA:  (*Embarrassed.*) You'll want some tea.

ANSUYA: I'll get it, Amma.

CHITRA: (*Callously.*) What happened to the big painting on this wall?

(*Sudden silence. They look at each other in embarrassment.*)

AMRITA: (*Lying, not convincingly.*) It's gone for being restored.

ANSUYA: Amma! Why don't you tell her the truth?

(*Pause.*)

It was sold in an auction.

CHITRA: Why?

ANSUYA: (*Glaring.*) We needed the money.

CHITRA: (*Looking around.*) Even the chandeliers are gone? You must have got a lot of money for those, ji. How much?

(*Another uncomfortable pause. Deepak is particularly uneasy.*)

ANSUYA: (*Trying to control herself.*) We did not. We didn't even get a tenth of what they were worth.

CHITRA: The painting—how much did it bring?

DEEPAK: (*Sternly.*) Ma!

(*Chitra is quiet.*)

AMRITA: You must be feeling tired and dusty. You will both want to bathe after such a long journey. I'll ask the cook to bring two *baltis* of hot water.

CHITRA: Baltis, Didi? What happened to the boilers?

ANSUYA: They too were sold—by mistake.

DEEPAK: For heavens sake, Ma. Stop this crude talk.

CHITRA: *Lekin Didi, aap ko yeh sab karne ki kya zaroorat hai? Aapke pas to itni millen hain, itni zamin hai!*

ANSUYA: (*Containing herself bravely.*) The mills and the lands are sold.

DEEPAK: (*With finality.*) Ma!

(*Turning around to the others with a smile.*)

I say, how are we going to celebrate Diwali with this war and the blackout and everything?

(*Enthusiastically, to Ansuya.*)

Let's think of something, yaar. Tell you what, I'll quickly have a bath and then we'll go down to the Mall, all right?

AMRITA: (*To Chitra.*) Chitra, how do you like living in Bombay?

CHITRA: I like it very much, ji. There are so many parties. We're invited out a lot because Deepak is doing so well. His boss says that he is the smartest boy they have had in years.

AMRITA: (*Genuinely proud.*) Deepak was always so intelligent.

CHITRA:    He makes one thousand, two hundred and eighty-six rupees per month, Didi!

DEEPAK:    (*Glaring.*) Ma!

CHITRA:    Just look at him, getting embarrassed before his own family. And his name was in the papers the other day.

MAMU:    Yes, you sent us the cutting.

DEEPAK:    (*Embarrassed.*) Trust her, sending cuttings to the whole world.

AMRITA:    (*Genuinely pleased.*) She's proud of you, son.

CHITRA:    (*In a hushed voice.*) We rushed here, Didi, because Deepak's company is bidding for a licence, and the big Government uffsar is here, in Simla.

AMRITA:    Who?

DEEPAK:    P.N. Rai, Aunty. He is the Secretary in the Ministry. He hasn't given us an appointment in Delhi for weeks.

CHITRA:    If Rai Saheb says 'yes,' Deepak's company will get the licence. And he's a friend of yours, Didi.

AMRITA:    Of course! Bunty is coming over this evening. Deepak will meet him.

CHITRA:    Bunty?

DEEPAK:    That's what Mr Rai's friends call him, Ma.

CHITRA:    Didi, will you also put in a word?

AMRITA:    Once he meets Deepak, it won't be necessary. Such a charming boy.

CHITRA:    Oh, thank you, Didi!
           (*Deepak smiles gratefully.*)

MAMU:    (*To Deepak, confidentially.*) Tell us, Deepak, will your company have to bribe him for the licence?

DEEPAK:    (*Taken aback.*) I . . . I . . . I say, what sort of question is that?

AMRITA:    Oh, Karan, you're impossible! (*To Chitra.*)
           Come dear, you should wash and get comfortable. And I shall send you tea upstairs.

CHITRA:    Thank you, Didi.
           (*Chitra and Deepak leave. Ansuya, sensing that she has hurt her mother, goes up to her.*)

AMRITA:    (*In tears.*) Why did you have to go and blabber about the auction? I would have slowly told her in my own way.

MAMU:    But Chitra knew the moment she stepped into the house.

ANSUYA:    What difference does it make, Amma, what she thinks? We have to learn to live without our mills and our lands.

(*Pause.*)

And now, even this house will be gone.

AMRITA:    (*Hysterically.*) No. It won't.

ANSUYA:    (*As if she is comforting a child.*) We can't afford it, Amma.

AMRITA:    (*In a dream.*) It's the only beautiful thing we have.

(*Musing.*)

When your father brought me here for the first time, how everyone fussed over us. You were born here, and this is where you spent your happiest days. It is for your children and their children.

(*Uncomfortable pause, while Mamu watches Ansuya closely, looking her up and down*)

MAMU:    And in whose honour are we all dressed up today?

ANSUYA:    (*Blushing.*) I thought it was Diwali, and we were having visitors—so I decided to wear a sari.

MAMU:    Achcha, I'm off to the Mall.

AMRITA:    Why don't you pick up some whiskey for this evening?

(*Mamu and Ansuya exchange glances.*)

MAMU:    Whiskey?

AMRITA:    Scotch.

(*Mamu and Ansuya again look at each other.*)

ANSUYA:    Amma, it's expensive.

MAMU:    Why can't he drink Indian whiskey?

AMRITA:    (*With finality.*) No. Scotch.

(*Exit Amrita. Mamu shrugs his shoulders, exchanges a glance with Ansuya and leaves. Pause. Deepak enters from the other side. He sneezes.*)

ANSUYA:    You poor thing!

DEEPAK:    (*Sneezing.*) I swear, yaar, it's a weird cat. I just ran into the non-sleeper. There it stood, quiet, composed, with a disapproving look; it watched me with a cruel expression, as if it were watching a mouse.

ANSUYA:    I sometimes think it has more life and free spirit than any of us.

(*Pause. She moves away to the window.*)

You know, Deepak, I'm angry with you.

DEEPAK:    Arre . . . Why?

ANSUYA:    I thought you came to Simla to see me. What's this about Rai Saheb and licences?

DEEPAK:    I *have* come to Simla to see you, Anu.
           (*Goes up to her.*)
  But then I discovered that Rai Saheb was also up here, and I told Ma,
  why not combine business with pleasure.

ANSUYA:    And I'm 'pleasure,' am I?

DEEPAK:    No, yaar. I didn't mean it like that.

ANSUYA:    What *did* you mean?

DEEPAK:    I say, yaar, don't be upset. Ma blabbered it out. I meant to
           slowly . . .

ANSUYA:    Stop blaming your mother for everything.

DEEPAK:    Ma's too much, yaar. She is more ambitious for me than even
           I am for me. Sometimes I get tired of her going on and on about me,
           even before perfect strangers. Why, on the way up to Simla, we
           stopped for breakfast at . . .what's that place called?

ANSUYA:    At Barog?

DEEPAK:    Yes.

ANSUYA:    (*Laughing.*) Everyone stops there!

DEEPAK:    There she was, mother dear, at Barog, whispering to the
           waiter, making sure her little boy's puri-alu were nice and hot. Let
           the rest of the world eat it cold, but for her little boy, it has to be
           nice and hot!
           (*He takes a deep breath.*)
  Anu, sometimes she smothers me so that I can hardly breathe.
           (*Pause.*)

ANSUYA:    I am sorry. It is just that I've been so looking forward to your
           coming. I have been counting the days.

DEEPAK:    So, tell me?

ANSUYA:    I wait for your letters. You don't know what it is like here. I'm
           tired of Amma and Mamu going on and on about the good old days.
           Honestly, sometimes I feel like going to bed at eight o'clock in the
           evening.

DEEPAK:    Oh, I say, there's the old radio.
           (*And he goes towards it.*)
  Shall we put it on?
           (*He examines the knobs.*)

ANSUYA:    (*Embarrassed.*) We only have old things. Mamu and Amma still
           cling to them, and try to hold on to the past.
           (*She laughs sadly. Deepak turns the radio on. Soft, romantic music is*

*heard, from one of the films of the early 1960s. Deepak goes to the window and takes a deep breath.)*

DEEPAK:    You know, Anu, I can still smell the one summer I spent in this house as a boy.

ANSUYA:    And you have grown up and become an important man . . .

DEEPAK:    *Arre chhodo!*

ANSUYA:    . . . and we've stayed the same. Even this house . . .

(*Realizing.*)

. . . oops!

DEEPAK:    What about the house?

ANSUYA:    I'm not supposed to say it.

DEEPAK:    Say what?

ANSUYA:    Well, everyone knows it anyway, and I can't hide anything from you. Even this house is up for sale.

(*Trying to laugh.*)

'The End,' as they say in the pictures.

DEEPAK:    Why?

ANSUYA:    (*Irritated.*) To pay our debts—what do you think, for our health?

(*Pause.*)

DEEPAK:    But the house need not be sold, you know.

ANSUYA:    Don't talk about it before Amma.

DEEPAK:    About what?

ANSUYA:    About the house.

DEEPAK:    You shouldn't have to sell it. (*Suddenly.*)

I'll tell you what!

ANSUYA:    What?

DEEPAK:    (*Speaking like a professional manager.*) Why not convert it into an exclusive season hotel? It is the perfect spot—Jakhoo Hill, the highest point in Simla, isn't it? 'Jakhoo Hotel for the discerning.' It would cost a bit to refurnish, but I'm sure we could get a loan from the bank. Give it to a professional company to manage it. 'Jakhoo Hotel, managed by the Taj.' The Oberois have the Cecil and the Clarks, but I'm sure there couldn't be enough hotel rooms here during the season. And I'm sure the Taj people would love to get their hands on a property like this. In fact, I know some of their senior chaps. I can speak to them. It will be the perfect answer for you. Open it in April and close it in October, and you could use it for the rest of the year. And, I tell you, in two years, you could pay back all your debts and keep the house, too.

ANSUYA:   Amma would never agree.

DEEPAK:   You must speak to her, yaar.

ANSUYA:   She won't.

DEEPAK:   All right, then I will.

ANSUYA:   (*Softly.*) Don't ! Don't you see this house means all that is beautiful and happy in her life—the gaiety of her younger days.

(*Long, embarrassed pause.*)

Deepak?

DEEPAK:   Huh?

ANSUYA:   Tell me about Bombay?

DEEPAK:   What about Bombay?

ANSUYA:   Does Bombay have a big heart?

DEEPAK:   Eh?

(*Ansuya excitedly goes and picks up the guidebook from the shelf and reads.*)

ANSUYA:   Tell me about Chowpatty and Malabar Hill and . . .

(*Deliberately.*) . . .

Cum-bal-la Hill! How nice the names sound. Ma-la-bar Hill, Cum-bal-la Hill!

(*She pronounces the names by elongating the 'a' vowel and she gets enormous pleasure in doing so.*)

DEEPAK:   Bombay is like any other city, yaar.

ANSUYA:   Bombay is not mean?

(*Deepak is puzzled.*)

If you scold a servant here, the whole town gets to know by the evening. As we sit here, they are gossiping about our house.

DEEPAK:   But Anu, Bombay can be heartless and indifferent.

ANSUYA:   I'd rather have the indifference than our great hospitality, which suffocates you in the end. You don't have Mrs Kumar…(*and she mimics.*) . . . 'I wonder what's wrong with that girl,' or Mrs Mehra … 'Arre, what a fast girl!' I dream of going to Bombay and those places that have such musical names!

(*She sings.*)

Cum-bal-la Hill, Ma-la-bar Hill, Cum-bal-la Hill . . .

(*And she's lost.*)

DEEPAK:   Wake up, Miss Malik, we're on Jakhoo Hill, Simla, and not Cumballa Hill, Bombay. It is Diwali and what are we going to do?

ANSUYA:   Oh Deepak, what can we do? There's a war on. There's a total blackout.

DEEPAK:   Why don't we light one candle and one *phuljari* and celebrate our own, secret Diwali on the verandah after dark—just the two of us?

ANSUYA:   Shall we?

DEEPAK:   Come on, Ansu, just one candle and a few phuljaris!

ANSUYA:   Oh, Deepak, you are going to bring Diwali into this house!

(*Deepak goes close to her.*)

I am so glad you are here.

(*He puts his arm around her. She puts her head on his shoulder.*)

DEEPAK:   Oh, Ansu . . .

(*They embrace.*)

ANSUYA:   I have missed you.

(*They kiss.*)

DEEPAK:   Me too!

(*Long kiss.*)

ANSUYA:   Oh Deepak!

(*Fade.*)

# Act Three

✦✦✦

[*Stage Centre. Spotlight on Karan, the narrator.*]

KARAN:   A Moorish proverb says, 'Every beetle is a gazelle in the eyes of its mother.' Deepak is not your ordinary beetle, and between you and me, neither is he a gazelle. But what matters is that to Chitra, he is a gazelle. Oh, what power is motherhood! If a son is not careful, he can easily grow pale under its weight. The father? The father is merely a banker provided by nature. Seriously, isn't the mother–son bond a paradox? It needs the most intense love from the mother, yet this very love must help the son become free and grow away from the mother.

    (*Pause. Picks up the Bombay guidebook left on the table by Ansuya.*)
Is it surprising that Ansu was attracted to Deepak? After all, he was handsome, he was doing well, and he lived in Bombay. She yearned for the voicelessness of the big city. A great city can be a great solitude. Ansu wanted to disappear in a crowd of strangers. A big city may be squalid, even callous, but it is also more tolerant of our fellow men.

    (*Pause.*)
In the scenes that follows, I regret that you will not see Mamu at his best. But then, jealousy humiliates us and exacts a heavy price.

    (*As the lights come on slowly, Karan looks at his watch.*)
It is six-thirty in the evening. Dusk has set in, which is not unusual for Simla at this time of the year. It has been raining intermittently since the afternoon. There is no further news from the front, but the radio bulletin at 6.00 p.m. said that President Kennedy in America has offered to send equipment and supplies to India. This should lift the morale of our jawans in the Eastern sector.

    (*Pause.*)
As you can see, the living room of 9 Jakhoo Hill looks visibly different. It is cheerful and bright and there is a festive feeling in the air. Something about that boy: he has infected everyone in the house with his bright good humour, even the Mali, who has just arranged those flowers over the fireplace. You can tell that Rai Saheb is expected from the bottle of Scotch whiskey which is conspicuous on the table there

on my left, surrounded by glasses and some bottles of Indian whiskey. Everyone is in his room, dressing up. But wait, what is Mamu doing, pacing about frantically?

(*Mamu is pacing up and down. Lights change. He bumps into Ansuya.*)

MAMU: (*Frantic.*) Where have you been?

ANSUYA: (*Cool.*) In and out.

MAMU: With Deepak?

(*She nods.*)

MAMU: Why does everything have to change just because he has come?

ANSUYA: I feel so happy!

MAMU: We were happy before he came.

ANSUYA: He is so alive.

MAMU: (*Defensively.*) What about us, Ansu? We were alive together, weren't we?

ANSUYA: This is different, Mamu. Only my mind is alive when I'm with you. With Deepak, my whole being is awake. And I can't control myself. It is as if I am being pulled.

MAMU: Ansuya, you can't . . .

(*Loudly.*)

Oh no!

ANSUYA: (*Concerned.*) What is the matter?

MAMU: I've got something in my eye.

ANSUYA: What is it? Sit down, Mamu.

(*He sits down on the sofa.*)

Let me see.

MAMU: It's in my left eye.

(*She sits on the arm of the sofa and helps him.*)

ANSUYA: Don't move . . . keep still . . . now. There, does that feel better?

MAMU: (*Nods.*) My eyes are not the same as they used to be.

(*She begins to get up.*)

I like holding your hand, Ansu. It feels so warm.

(*He kisses her hand.*)

Ansuya, there's something I've been wanting to tell you . . .

ANSUYA: Sh . . . don't say anything. Keep still, Mamu.

MAMU: Please Ansuya, this concerns you and me . . .

ANSUYA: Mamu?

MAMU: I've been meaning to tell you for some time . . .

ANSUYA: Mamu!

MAMU:    I must tell you now . . .

ANSUYA:   No!

> (*Pause.*)

You've been good to me, Mamu. I don't want to spoil it. It is Diwali, I'm happy.

MAMU:    (*Sad.*) Well, I am not.

> (*Pause.*)

Look at me. I've lived all my life with books and ideas. And here I am, stuck with shallow people like the Rai Sahebs and Deepaks of this world. I have no one to talk to . . . except you, and even you are drawing away from me. I am beginning to feel like a complete failure.

ANSUYA:   You say it as though it were my fault.

MAMU:    No, no, my sweet Ansuya.

> (*He grabs her by the arm.*)

It's just that I can't bear to lose you.

ANSUYA:   Sh . . . Deepak and the others will come in.

MAMU:    Why has Deepak come?

> (*Sounds of footsteps.*)

ANSUYA:   Mamu, please!

> (*Breaking away from him.*)

There's Deepak!

> (*Enter Deepak. He is suited and booted, the picture of confidence, but he is a little disconcerted by what he sees.*)

DEEPAK:   I . . . I didn't mean to interrupt.

ANSUYA:   You did not. We were just waiting for everyone. Do sit down, Deepak.

DEEPAK:   (*Uneasily.*) Well, ah . . .

> (*To Mamu.*)

Karan Uncle, how do you like the university?

MAMU:    Which university?

DEEPAK:   Where you teach.

MAMU:    What do you want me to say?

DEEPAK:   Well . . . ah . . .

MAMU:    Are you making polite conversation, or do you really want to know?

DEEPAK:   Well . . .

MAMU:    If you want to know the truth, I hate it.

DEEPAK:   I'm sorry.

MAMU:     'Sorry?' Why are you 'sorry?' Do you want to know why?

DEEPAK:   Yes.

MAMU:     No, you don't.

DEEPAK:   (*With a good natured smile.*) I don't?

MAMU:     Deepak, you are ambitious. All you want to do is to get on in life. You don't really want to know about the dark side of things.

ANSUYA:   (*Uncomfortably.*) Mamu, this is not the place . . .

MAMU:     You are not even aware what the words you use really mean. Do you really care what 'love–hate,' 'beautiful–ugly,' 'true–false' are all about?

ANSUYA:   Mamu, please!

MAMU:     (*Ignoring her.*) There's nothing wrong with that. But, let me give you a tip. Don't waste your time over small talk. Do you really care about my university?'

DEEPAK:   (*Puzzled.*) Well . . .

MAMU:     Of course you don't. So then, let's talk about what you really care about.

DEEPAK:   (*Affably.*) Certainly.

MAMU:     Let's talk about Ansuya.

ANSUYA:   Mamu, for God's sake.

MAMU:     Tell us about your interest in Ansuya.

DEEPAK:   (*Suspiciously.*) What about her?

MAMU:     Well, I thought it would be nice to know how you feel about her. I am her uncle, after all.

ANSUYA:   (*In tears.*) Mamu, you're spoiling everything.

MAMU:     I don't want to embarrass you. I'm fascinated by the methodology of your mind . . . by the pragmatic calculation which a successful business executive makes in taking a decision about another human being. It's purely an intellectual interest, mind you, nothing personal . . . an interest in a certain type of human being, who is rational, self-interested and—what's the word…optimising.

DEEPAK:   (*With a puzzled smile.*) You don't seem to like me or the work I do.

MAMU:     Deepak, I am fascinated by the business world and how it works.

DEEPAK:   Sir, I am proud of what I do and the company I work for. You may think what you like, but I believe we care more about our people than many academics do for their students.

MAMU:     Hold on . . .

DEEPAK:     (*Continuing.*) I mean, we care about our customers, our suppliers,
            our employees, because for us it is a matter of survival. I can't remember
            a single professor of mine at college who cared for me in the same
            way.

MAMU:    Now, hold on . . .
            (*Knocking at the door. Ansuya is relieved.*)

ANSUYA:  There is Rai Saheb.
            (*Shouting.*)
            Amma, Rai Saheb is here!
            (*Ansuya opens the door. Rai Saheb comes in, looking tweedy, distinguished,
            and the pukka 'brown sahib.' Chitra is dressed to kill.*)

AMRITA:    (*Off-stage.*) Oh no, is he here already? And I'm not quite ready
            (*Entering with a bowl of flowers.*)
            Bunty, Happy Diwali!

RAI SAHEB:  Happy Diwali!

AMRITA:    Just smell these gorgeous October roses! Aren't they lovely?

RAI SAHEB:  Not half as lovely as you, my dear! I'm not early, am I?

AMRITA:    No. You know how it gets dark early in Simla these days. Bunty,
            I want you to meet Chitra, a family friend of ours from Lahore. And
            this is her son, Deepak.

CHITRA:    (*Manufacturing her biggest smile.*) Namaste, Rai Saheb! *Aap ke
            baare me to bahut suna hai!*

RAI SAHEB:  Nothing good, I hope!

DEEPAK:     (*Shaking hands.*) Hello, I'm Kapur, sir.

AMRITA:    (*To Rai Saheb.*) Deepak is a fine young man, Bunty, doing
            famously in a company in Bombay.

RAI SAHEB:  Which company?

DEEPAK:    TCK, sir.

ANSUYA:  Deepak's from the *big* city, Bunty Uncle.

RAI SAHEB:  Well, we are not exactly villagers.

ANSUYA:  Delhi is a village by comparison.

AMRITA:    (*To Rai Saheb.*) Chitra here grew up with me in Lahore; her
            father was Papa's legal aide, and they lived in our compound at
            Lahore.

RAI SAHEB:  (*To Ansuya.*) Ansu, my dear, you are looking positively radiant.

AMRITA:    You will have your usual, Bunty? With soda?

RAI SAHEB:  A splash of soda, thank you.

MAMU:    Scotch for the Brown Sahib.

AMRITA:   And for you, Deepak?

DEEPAK:   The same, thank you, aunty.

AMRITA:   Chitra?

CHITRA:   Tea for me, ji.

AMRITA:   Karan?

MAMU:   Indian whiskey with water will do for me, thank you. I'll get the drinks. (*He gets up to make the drinks.*)

AMRITA:   (*Frowning at Mamu.*) You know my brother. He must be different.

ANSUYA:   I'll get the tea, Amma.
          (*Exit.*)

AMRITA:   (*Graciously changing the subject.*) It has been an unusually damp October, especially after such a lovely summer.

RAI SAHEB:   (*Winking naughtily.*) Do you know, I caught Bubbles at it last Friday? Imagine, Bubbles Chopra, wearing chappals on the Mall! Poor man, he was mortified when he saw me, and tried to sneak away. I went up to him and I said, 'Could I buy you a pair of shoes, old man?'
          (*And he roars with laughter. Deepak and then Chitra join in.*)

MAMU:   (*Mimicking him.*) 'I say, old chap, what is wrong with chappals?'
          (*Amrita frowns at him.*)

RAI SAHEB:   Nothing ... in your bedroom.
          (*Continues to laugh.*)

MAMU:   The whole country wears chappals, Rai Saheb.
          (*Ansuya enters with a tray of tea. Deepak begins to sneeze.*)

ANSUYA:   Mamu's cat!

CHITRA:   The cat will be the death of this boy.

AMRITA:   Poor Deepak! Karan, you and your cat. Lock it up!

MAMU:   What can I do if she sneaks out? She watches Deepak like a mouse.

RAI SAHEB:   (*Laughing.*) Ha! Ha! Like a mouse. If we cross Karan and his cat, it would improve Karan, but it would deteriorate the cat. Ho, ho, ho!

AMRITA:   Really, Bunty!
          (*To Deepak.*)
          Are you better, son? You know this boy, Bunty, he is doing brilliantly in Bombay.

CHITRA:   (*Interrupting.*) Rai Saheb, this boy never opened a book in his life and he always came first.

DEEPAK:   (*Embarrassed.*) Ma, please!

CHITRA:     (*Not to be stopped.*) Rai Saheb, *jab yeh chhota sa tha, tab se bahut seedha tha. Hamesha apna doodh peeta tha, school se seedha ghar laut aata tha,* not like other boys. He always combed his hair . . .

DEEPAK:     Ma!

CHITRA:     Listen to him, ji. After all I do for him. You know, he likes rice. So on Sundays, I make him Basmati rice, which costs five rupees a kilo, while I eat the one rupee, *char anna* variety from the ration shop. And this is my reward, ji.

DEEPAK:     (*Almost screaming.*) Ma!
            (*To Rai Saheb.*)
            I am sorry, sir.

MAMU:       Deepak and his Ma!

ANSUYA:     (*Giving Mamu a dirty look.*) Mamu!

RAI SAHEB:  (*Patronizingly.*) Hmm. What school did you go to, young man?

DEEPAK:     (*Charmingly.*) I went to St. Mary's in Bombay, sir.

MAMU:       You don't have to say 'sir' all the time. This isn't an office, you know.

AMRITA:     (*Rescuing Deepak.*) He's just a well-brought-up boy. He respects his elders.

MAMU:       Why don't you say 'sir' with a question mark at the end? Like this: 'Sir?' Interesting, isn't it? 'Sir?'... leaves a doubt in the mind.

AMRITA:     Stop it, Karan Chand.

DEEPAK:     Well, ah . . .

RAI SAHEB:  (*Patronizingly.*) What does your father do?
            (*Uneasy pause.*)

DEEPAK:     (*Defensively.*) Oh, he is a businessman.

RAI SAHEB:  And what is his business?

CHITRA:     (*After a brief pause.*) Buying and selling, ji.

RAI SAHEB:  Buying and selling what?
            (*Another uncomfortable pause.*)

DEEPAK:     (*Crestfallen.*) He runs a general store.

RAI SAHEB:  (*Contemptuously.*) Oh, a shopkeeper. Where is his shop?

CHITRA:     Deepak lives on Malabar Hill with the gentry.

RAI SAHEB:  Yes, I see, but where is the shop?

DEEPAK:     (*Quietly.*) At Ghatkopar, sir.

CHITRA:     But we live in Deepak's big flat on Malabar Hill.

RAI SAHEB:  (*Suddenly beaming at Chitra.*) On Malabar Hill? And where have *you* been hiding yourself, my dear? Here we have a beauty in our midst and no one knows about it.

CHITRA:  (*Blushing.*) Oh, I just came this morning, ji.

RAI SAHEB:  (*Flirting.*) Well you must come to the Club and meet everyone.

CHITRA:  (*Gushing.*) Oh yes ji, I'd love to meet, ji.

RAI SAHEB:  (*Putting his arm around her.*) How about a drink for you, my dear? Don't tell me you are going to keep drinking tea the whole evening.

CHITRA:  (*Reluctantly.*) Well, you know Rai Saheb, I don't drink really.

RAI SAHEB:  (*Flirting.*) There's always a first time. Come along, my dear, just to keep us company.

CHITRA:  (*Giggling.*) Well, if you say so ji, just a tiny bit.

RAI SAHEB:  Come!

(*And he takes Chitra with him towards the drinks table. He still has his arm around her.*)

Come, we'll go to the Club this evening. (*Chitra giggles.*)

It's settled, then.

ANSUYA:  Let's go outside, Deepak. It's dark now.

DEEPAK:  (*Reluctantly.*) Later, Ansuya.

ANSUYA:  (*Feverishly.*) But its's lovely outside. Come!

RAI SAHEB:  (*Smiling.*) Ansu, my dear, why not celebrate it with a drink?

ANSUYA:  (*Crossly.*) No.

RAI SAHEB:  Let's have some music.

(*To Chitra.*)

You do dance, don't you, my dear?

CHITRA:  You can teach me, ji.

RAI SAHEB:  Amrita my dear, don't you have anything danceable? How about a fox-trot?

AMRITA:  I'll put on the music.

(*As the music comes on, Rai Saheb swings and does a few steps, humming to himself and starts demonstrating the steps to Chitra.*)

RAI SAHEB:  Amrita, why don't you bring your guests to the party at the Government House?

(*Silence.*)

AMRITA:  (*Hurt.*) Is there a party at the Government House?

RAI SAHEB:  Yes, tomorrow evening.

AMRITA:  (*Hurt.*) We haven't been invited.

RAI SAHEB:   (*Covering up.*) Really? Not possible. Someone's slipped up.

      (*Rai Saheb takes Chitra in his arms and begins to dance with her.*)

AMRITA:   Besides, those parties aren't worth going to any more.

CHITRA:   You move so nicely, ji.

RAI SAHEB:   Just follow me.

CHITRA:   (*Hesitantly.*) Oh, I don't know these steps, ji . . .

RAI SAHEB:   It's easy, see. One, two, three; one, two, three . . .

CHITRA:   (*Getting into the swing.*) Oh! You move so smoothly. You make it so easy.

RAI SAHEB:   (*Seductively.*) I like the way you move.

CHITRA:   I like the way you move, too.

MAMU:   *They* like the way they move.

AMRITA:   Aren't they cute, like youngsters?

      (*Rai Saheb now holds Chitra closer and they dance tightly together.*)

RAI SAHEB:   You are warm, my dear.

CHITRA:   You too.

RAI SAHEB:   I like it.

CHITRA:   Me too.

AMRITA:   They are dancing like they've danced together before.

MAMU:   It's a familiar game . . . they both know it.

RAI SAHEB:   You're not shy.

CHITRA:   I'm . . . I'm not?

MAMU:   It's an old ritual . . . as old as man and woman.

DEEPAK:   (*Shocked.*) What! Don't say that about my mother.

MAMU:   Are you surprised?

DEEPAK:   (*Angry.*) Yes.

ANSUYA:   Deepak, let's go out on the verandah now. Come!

MAMU:   (*Desperately.*) Ansu, please don't go out!

ANSUYA:   Mamu, what's wrong?

MAMU:   (*Frantic.*) I don't know what's come over me. I'm afraid something . . . something is going to happen.

AMRITA:   What's wrong, Karan?

ANSUYA:   Come on, Deepak! Let's go!

MAMU:   (*Pleading.*) Please don't go out, Ansu!

DEEPAK:   (*Sneezing.*) Let's go, yaar! I need to breathe . . . away from the cat.

ANSUYA:   (*Singing.*) Cum-bal-la Hill! Ma-la-bar Hill!

      (*Exit Deepak and Ansuya.*)

AMRITA:    Karan, you are behaving very strangely.

MAMU:    Don't you see, she is vulnerable. She has been lonely for so long. Anyone, anyone who comes along could . . . Oh, the hell with it!

*(Stomps off to his room.)*

RAI SAHEB:    *(Dancing close.)* Let's go out for a while.

CHITRA:    Mm . . . if you wish.

RAI SAHEB:    Let's go.

*(They stop dancing and go to the others.)*

Amrita, my dear, we'll nip over to the Club and I'll bring your lovely guest back soon . . . very soon.

*(Fade on Amrita alone on stage, as she switches off the music, picks up a pack of cards and starts playing Solitaire. Spot on Deepak and Ansuya in the veranda.)*

ANSUYA:    *(Sullen.)* You were really 'lagaoing' an impression on him, weren't you?

DEEPAK:    If I get this licence, it will be a big thing for my career, yaar.

ANSUYA:    *(Sulking.)* You are ambitious!

DEEPAK:    *(Appeasingly.)* What the hell, yaar!

ANSUYA:    Be yourself!

*(Pause.)*

DEEPAK:    *(Pensive.)* I suppose you are right.

ANSUYA:    *(Gently.)* And don't be ashamed of your father.

*(Pause.)*

Come, don't look sad. You have too much dignity.

DEEPAK:    *(Suddenly energetic.)* Let's light the candle, yaar.

*(They light a candle and then one sparkler each. As the candle and sparklers are lit, lights are slowly dimmed.)*

ANSUYA:    *(Glowing.)* Oh Deepak, it's beautiful!

DEEPAK:    And now the sparklers.

ANSUYA:    *(Vivaciously.)* Deepak, your mood is infectious. I'm already happy.

DEEPAK:    Give me a match, yaar.

*(Deepak starts lighting sparklers and gives them to Ansuya.)*

DEEPAK:    Hang on . . . I'll light this.

*(He lights another one, while Ansuya makes patterns in the air with the sparkler.)*

ANSUYA:    I don't think I'll be able to sleep tonight.

*(Deepak is busy lighting diyas. She sings.)*

Cum-bal-la Hill, Cum-bal-la Hill!

> (*Looking out.*)

Here I am, in this beautiful world, with the stars and the smell of the pine trees and the hills. Why can't I be this happy all the time?

> (*Pause.*)

Deepak, you know, you remind me of my father. You smile like him. You have his same sense of life . . . and hope.

DEEPAK:  (*Pensive.*) How life changes! You were the spoiled daughter of a rich father, remember?

ANSUYA:  (*Wistfully.*) No rich father, no spoiled daughter, no house, nothing. It's all over!

DEEPAK:  (*Suddenly serious.*) Ansuya, come with me to Bombay.

ANSUYA:  (*Stunned.*) To Bombay?

DEEPAK:  Yes . . .

ANSUYA:  (*Overjoyed.*) Do you mean it?

DEEPAK:  Yes.

ANSUYA:  Oh, but I couldn't. What will they say?

DEEPAK:  (*Hesitantly.*) I have a large flat and . . .

ANSUYA:  Do you really think I could go?

> (*Frowning.*)

But what will I do?

DEEPAK:  You can work. You could start by converting this house into a hotel. I'll fix up appointments with the hotel people. I can see it, 'Jakhoo Hotel.'

ANSUYA:  (*Frowning.*) But I can't do anything. I can't even type.

DEEPAK:  I'll help you.

> (*In a professional manager's tone.*)

We shall ask them to restore the house and the entrance will look just as it did fifty years ago. They'll put in modern bathrooms, of course. We can position it as an exclusive, low volume, high margin venture.

ANSUYA:  (*Joyfully.*) I don't know what those words mean, but it sounds so exciting, Deepak! I'll ask Amma. I shall work hard in Bombay.

> (*Going close to him.*)

Oh, it is a beautiful dream.

DEEPAK:  (*Holding her in his arms.*) It's going to come true.

ANSUYA:  You mean it!

DEEPAK:  Come here.

> (*They kiss.*)

ANSUYA:   I still can't believe it.

> (*They kiss again.*)

Come, let's go back to the others.

DEEPAK:   Shh! Not yet.

ANSUYA:   I'm afraid of your mother.

DEEPAK:   Come, let's go to your room.

ANSUYA:   It's late. It isn't right.

DEEPAK:   Ansu, I need you in Bombay. It's lonely with just Ma and . . . and sometimes she gets too much. She sits on my back like a monkey. She's turned my father into a vegetable. And she's going to do it to me too.

ANSUYA:   Shh!

DEEPAK:   I need you to . . . to save me from her.

> (*Pause.*)

Come, let's go to your room.

ANSUYA:   No.

DEEPAK:   Come on, yaar.

ANSUYA:   Do you really think we should?

DEEPAK:   Yes.

ANSUYA:   (*Getting up to go.*) I don't trust myself. I . . . I mean, I'm so drunk with all this happiness and . . .

DEEPAK:   (*Softly.*) Let's go.

ANSUYA:   I can't believe this is happening.

DEEPAK:   (*Tenderly.*) Everything is going to be all right.

> (*Exuent and fade. Lights come up on the drawing room. It is two hours later. Rai Saheb and Chitra have returned.*)

AMRITA:   How was the Club?

RAI SAHEB:   (*Uncomfortably.*) Fine, fine.

> (*Looks bored.*)

I say, I need another drink. (*Pours himself one.*)

Come on, let's do something. Let's play a game.

AMRITA:   Oh Bunty, you and your silly games.

CHITRA:   Didi, *bachche kahan gai?*

AMRITA:   They were on the verandah awhile ago.

MAMU:   What could be keeping them?

RAI SAHEB:   What shall we play?

AMRITA:   They must have gone for a walk. It's stopped raining.

CHITRA:   (*Frantically.*) My Deepak! He'll catch a chill.

RAI SAHEB:   Or the cat will catch Deepak.

CHITRA:    Ji?

MAMU:    Cats are known to have killed people.

CHITRA:    Hey Ram!

AMRITA:    Stop it, the two of you!

CHITRA:    (*Nervously.*) My Deepak, he has disappeared. That boy will be the death of me.

AMRITA:    Calm down, they will be here soon.

MAMU:    (*To Amrita.*) You are too easy going, leaving them alone like that.

AMRITA:    Shame on you, Karan. A liberal person like you, talking like this.

MAMU:    Anything can happen between two young people.

RAI SAHEB:    My dear, that is the fun of being young. What's in a little hanky-panky . . .?

(*And he gives Chitra a whack on her bum.*)

CHITRA:    (*Giggling.*) Rai Saheb! You are naughty.

RAI SAHEB:    Come on, let me fill your glass, my darling.

CHITRA:    (*Slightly high.*) Just a tiny bit.

RAI SAHEB:    I know, we'll play charades.

MAMU:    Oh no!

(*Fade. Deepak and Ansuya emerge on the veranda, looking dishevelled.*)

DEEPAK:    Hurry, they will be looking for us.

ANSUYA:    I love you, Deepak.

DEEPAK:    Comb your hair. (*Nervous.*)
Here, use my comb.

ANSUYA:    (*Combing her hair.*) I don't want to go in. I want to stay with you.

DEEPAK:    What will they think, yaar? I told you we shouldn't have stayed in the bedroom for so long.

ANSUYA:    I love you, Deepak.

DEEPAK:    Come on!

(*Fade. Lights come up on the drawing room. The seating order for the next scene is important. It is vaguely a circle. Deepak and Ansuya enter. They take positions in a clockwise order as follows: Deepak, Chitra, Rai Saheb, Ansuya, Amrita and Mamu. Mamu will change his position midway, between Chitra and Rai Saheb.*)

RAI SAHEB:    So, it's decided. We're going to play 'Truth or Dare.'

AMRITA:    Here they are!

CHITRA:    (*To Deepak.*) Mere bachche!

RAI SAHEB:    (*With a smile.*) Your 'bachcha' is fine. You're both just in time. We were going to play 'Truth or Dare.'

AMRITA:    For heaven's sake, Bunty! It's a game girls play in boarding school.

DEEPAK:    (*To Rai Saheb.*) How do you play it?

RAI SAHEB:    Dinky, Chippy and their crowd play it all the time. We sit in a circle. You are asked, 'Truth or Dare?' If you choose 'truth,' you are asked a question and you must answer it truthfully.

DEEPAK:    And if it is 'dare?'

RAI SAHEB:    Then you are dared to do something. And we go round the room; the ones who put the questions go clockwise and those who reply go anti-clockwise.

DEEPAK:    Who starts?

RAI SAHEB:    You.

DEEPAK:    Me? (*Laughs.*)

All right.

(*Turns to Mamu.*)

Karan Uncle, Truth or Dare?

MAMU:    This is silly! I don't want to play.

AMRITA:    Come on, Karan, it's only a game.

MAMU:    No.

RAI SAHEB:    Be a sport, Karan Chand.

MAMU:    No.

RAI SAHEB:    Then it's your turn, Amrita.

AMRITA:    Me? Must you begin with me?

RAI SAHEB:    Yes, we are going anti-clockwise, remember?

AMRITA:    (*To Deepak.*) Then ask me an easy question, son.

DEEPAK:    All right, Aunty. Truth or Dare?

AMRITA:    Truth.

DEEPAK:    Let me think. All right Aunty, what do you want more than anything in the world?

(*Pause. Amrita thinks.*)

RAI SAHEB:    Come on, my dear.

AMRITA:    Let me think, Bunty.

(*Stark silence. All eyes are on Amrita. Suddenly, there are tears in Amrita's eyes.*)

AMRITA:    I . . . I don't want to lose this house.

RAI SAHEB:    Good! That was a truth. But only half a truth.

(*Amrita gets up, wipes her eyes, goes to the window.*)

AMRITA:    I've always loved to look out of this window. God knows, I love this house.

(*To Ansuya.*)

Your father and I used to sleep in the big room upstairs. I used to wake up, my heart full of happiness each morning. And I'd rush down and look out of this window. Once we were here in January and we were caught in a snowstorm. It was all white outside. Oh, Ansu, it was heaven!

(*Pause.*)

I wish I could forget the past. If there is one good thing left in our lives, it is this house.

DEEPAK:   Aunty, you could turn the house into an exclusive season hotel . . . just six months a year . . . and you could still enjoy it the rest of the time.

AMRITA:   My dear, forgive me. But I don't think that you know what you are talking about.

(*She bursts into tears.*)

DEEPAK:   I'm sorry, Aunty, I didn't mean to upset you . . .

ANSUYA:   Darling Amma, don't cry!

(*Goes to her and embraces her.*)

Nothing will happen to this house.

AMRITA:   (*Weeping.*) If only I had looked after things better . . .

ANSUYA:   (*Wiping her mother's tears.*) Shh . . . Amma!

(*Turns to the others.*)

RAI SAHEB:   I say, Ansuya, let's carry on with the game. It is your turn. Chitra my dear, your turn to ask the question.

CHITRA:   I pass.

RAI SAHEB:   What?

CHITRA:   Pass.

DEEPAK:   Ma, ask her a question!

CHITRA:   Oh, all right. *Haan* Ansuya, Truth or Dare?

ANSUYA:   Truth.

CHITRA:   What do you want more than anything in the world, Ansuya?

ANSUYA:   (*Matter-of-factly.*) I want to go to Bombay.

CHITRA:   Bombay? Why?

ANSUYA:   I don't have to answer that. I already gave my 'truth'.

RAI SAHEB:   She's right. It's Deepak's turn.

ANSUYA:   No, it's your turn, Bunty Uncle. You are on my right.

MAMU:   (*Shifting to the empty chair on Chitra's right.*) It's all right. I'll ask, Rai Saheb.

RAI SAHEB:     Wait, that isn't fair! That's not your position. You've moved.

MAMU:     It's your turn to ask a question and it's also your turn to reply. You can't very well ask yourself a question.

RAI SAHEB:     Oh, very well.

(*Pointing to Deepak.*)

But let him go first.

ANSUYA:     But it's not his turn.

DEEPAK:     (*Confidently.*) Certainly I'll go, sir.

RAI SAHEB:     (*Pointing to Ansuya.*) You ask him, my dear.

ANSUYA:     But it's not my turn to ask.

DEEPAK:     (*Decisively, to Ansuya.*) Come on, Anu, I'm ready.

ANSUYA:     Oh, all right.

(*Pause.*)

Truth or Dare?

DEEPAK:     Truth.

ANSUYA:     Deepak, what is it that you want more than anything in the world?

CHITRA:     Wait, I know the answer, ji.

RAI SAHEB:     Let him speak for himself, my dear.

CHITRA:     I'm his mother, after all. I should know.

MAMU:     That's the problem.

CHITRA:     What is the problem, ji?

RAI SAHEB:     Nothing.

(*To Deepak.*)

Answer the question.

DEEPAK:     Well, I want to be a success at my job.

RAI SAHEB:     False.

CHITRA:     It's true!

RAI SAHEB:     It's false.

CHITRA:     How do you know?

RAI SAHEB:     You can tell he's lying.

CHITRA:     You are calling my son a liar?

RAI SAHEB:     Ask him.

CHITRA:     *Kyon* Deepak, was it a lie?

ANSUYA:     Was it, Deepak?

DEEPAK:     (*Hesitating.*) Well . . .

RAI SAHEB:     (*Triumphantly.*) So, False! The turn stays on you.

(*Pause.*)

Well?

    (*Silence.*)

Well?

    (*Silence. To Ansuya.*)

Ask him again, dear.

ANSUYA:    Deepak, what do you want more than anything in the world?

DEEPAK:    You, of course.

CHITRA:    More than your mother?

DEEPAK:    That's not the question, Ma.

MAMU:    Well, in a sense it is. If you want Ansuya more than anything or anyone, then you do want her more than your mother.

DEEPAK:    (*Laughing.*) I'm not going to fall into that trap.

CHITRA:    How could you, Deepak?

DEEPAK:    Oh, I want you equally, Ma.

CHITRA:    *Rahne de, rahne de!* Just look at him. You know what my fault is, ji? I am too good. Even if I get slapped in return, I can't stop being good.

RAI SAHEB:    (*With irony.*) You're good, my dear.

MAMU:    Deepak's had his turn. It's Rai Saheb's turn to answer now.

RAI SAHEB:    Oh, very well.

MAMU:    Are you ready?

RAI SAHEB:    (*Nods.*) Hmm.

MAMU:    Truth or Dare?

RAI SAHEB:    Truth, of course.

MAMU:    Will you take a bribe in awarding the licence to Deepak's company?

    (*Stunned silence.*)

RAI SAHEB:    I say, what sort of nonsense is this? I don't have to answer this stupid question.

    (*Silence. He looks around for support.*)

Come on, what the hell's going on?

AMRITA:    (*Uncomfortably.*) Bunty, you certainly don't have to answer that question. I don't like this game.

MAMU:    He started the game, Didi.

RAI SAHEB:    I didn't think you would start insulting people.

AMRITA:    Stop this childish nonsense.

RAI SAHEB:    I don't have to stand this insolence.

MAMU:    It's part of the game.

DEEPAK:    Shall we stop the game, sir?

RAI SAHEB:    Shut up, boy! You're out of your depth.

MAMU:    Well?

ANSUYA:    Bunty Uncle, why don't you merely say 'no' or 'yes' and we'll move on?

RAI SAHEB:    But, but . . . This is preposterous!

MAMU:    What's preposterous?

RAI SAHEB:    It's a matter of principle.

MAMU:    What principle?

RAI SAHEB:    (*Pompously.*) Do you know whom you are speaking to? You are insulting the Government of India.

MAMU:    Ah . . . we are high and mighty, aren't we!

RAI SAHEB:    I say, this is supposed to be light-hearted stuff. We're meant to talk about secret love affairs and fun things like that.

MAMU:    You'd like that. You'll proudly tell us of your sexual escapades. We are not talking of Sunday morning bingo, or 'elevenses' with the memsahibs, or cocktails in the Green Room, Rai Saheb. We're talking of licenses and hard cash!

RAI SAHEB:    Steady on, old chap!

MAMU:    The hypocrisy of the bureaucrat!

RAI SAHEB:    We merely carry out policy.

MAMU:    Ah, but 'we' love the policy. It gives us the power to have the likes of Deepak grovel before us: 'Yes, sir,' 'No, sir.'

RAI SAHEB:    I admit it's awkward—this licencing business. But someone has to do it!

MAMU:    Ah, but it's such a profitable business!

RAI SAHEB:    Enough of this insolence! The answer to your question is "no"!
          (*Pause.*)
          All right! It is now my turn to ask you a question, my friend.

MAMU:    Wait a minute . . .

RAI SAHEB:    Not my fault that you changed positions. We're going clockwise, remember?

AMRITA:    Stop this game, you silly boys.

ANSUYA:    It is Mamu's turn.

MAMU:    We've had enough of this game. Why don't you play something else?

RAI SAHEB:    Don't be a coward, Karan.

MAMU:    No.

RAI SAHEB:    Just when it is getting interesting?

ANSUYA:   Come on, Mamu. It's only a game.

>(*Mamu senses the mood and reluctantly agrees.*)

MAMU:   (*Looking at Ansuya.*) All right, you asked for it.

RAI SAHEB:   Truth or Dare?

MAMU:   Truth.

RAI SAHEB:   Remember, Karan, if you don't speak the truth, the turn
stays on you. Ready?

>(*Mamu nods.*)

What is your biggest regret?

>(*Pause.*)

MAMU:   Er . . . that . . . um . . . that I'm not a good teacher.

RAI SAHEB:   False! You are a good teacher.

MAMU:   (*Protesting weakly.*) No . . . it's true . . . I read from the notes I
made fifteen years ago. My students don't care for me.

ANSUYA:   That's not true, Mamu. You are a great teacher.

MAMU:   Was.

RAI SAHEB:   So, 'False.' The turn stays on you, Karan. Don't lie this time.
It's going to get more difficult, old boy.

MAMU:   Don't 'old boy' me.

RAI SAHEB:   Ready?

>(*Mamu nods reluctantly.*)

What is your greatest wish?

MAMU:   Behold, ladies and gentlemen, before you is the portrait of a
failure. No, no . . . a classic failure. The question is: why do some
men succeed while others fail?

RAI SAHEB:   We don't need a lecture, Professor.

MAMU:   (*Ignoring him.*) Take my case, for example: a drowning man . . .

AMRITA:   What are you talking about, Karan?

RAI SAHEB:   He's been drinking?.

>(*To Mamu.*)

Don't be dramatic, dear boy. Just answer the question.

MAMU:   Shut up!

CHITRA:   (*Unbelieving.*) He told Rai Saheb to 'shut up'!

DEEPAK:   Shut up, Ma!

CHITRA:   (*Hurt.*) My son tells me to 'shut up?'

DEEPAK:   Shh!

MAMU:   (*Continuing as if there was no interruption.*) The Question is: Why
is Deepak a success and I a failure? A very good question. As a young

man, I stood first at the University; I got into the ICS. But I chose to become a scholar and to teach. Because I had ideals and I wanted to pass them on to young people. Today, I could have been a loathsome diplomat, perhaps even a junior ambassador to some minor country. At least, I would have had some respect. I feel cheated.

(*Pause.*)

What is the moral of the story? Don't have ideals. Go for worldly success.

(*Pause.*)

But, surely that isn't right? When a young person cannot stand the way things are, then he must question the social order. The world is unjust. There is such misery and pain. I wanted answers to those questions. And what did I become? A dusty professor, of no use to anyone.

ANSUYA:   That's not true, Mamu. You created a whole generation of idealistic young people.

MAMU:   No, my students only wanted to pass exams. All they did was to copy my lecture notes. Of what possible use is an armchair intellectual to the world? All talk and no action.

(*Bitterly.*)

The result? No one wants me anymore . . . except my cat.

ANSUYA:   That's not true, Mamu. You gave me all that's good in me.

RAI SAHEB:   This is against the rules of the game. You can't help him, Ansuya.

ANSUYA:   You don't understand. He needs me.

MAMU:   (*Calmly.*) Well, maybe that is the way it was meant to be. I sat here tonight on Diwali night, and I watched you, Ansuya. I watched you and Deepak. And I looked at myself. You were looking to the future, I was looking to the past. It finally snapped!

(*Pause.*)

Tell me, you wise people, what should I do with my life? Should I shoot myself?

RAI SAHEB:   Stop being dramatic.

AMRITA:   I don't like this game.

DEEPAK:   This is embarrassing.

RAI SAHEB:   It is sickening.

(*Realizing.*)

But he still hasn't answered the question.

Are you listening, Karan Chand? Answer the question.

MAMU:     (*Afraid.*) I . . . I'm not going to answer that question.
          (*The tempo increases.*)
ANSUYA:   I'm afraid, Amma. Let's stop the game, Bunty Uncle.
RAI SAHEB:   We can't wait all night, Professor Saheb.
MAMU:     No . . . no.
ANSUYA:   I think we've gone too far this time.
RAI SAHEB:   Well?
MAMU:     (*Looking at Amrita, then at Ansuya.*) I don't know . . . do we have
          to go through with this?
          (*Turning to Ansuya.*)
AMRITA:   (*Worried.*) What is going on?
ANSUYA:   I don't like what's going on.
RAI SAHEB:   Do you know what it is?
ANSUYA:   I don't like it.
DEEPAK:   (*Puzzled.*) What's going on, yaar?
ANSUYA:   (*Scared.*) Stop the game!
DEEPAK:   (*Worried.*) What the hell, yaar?
RAI SAHEB:   (*Silencing everyone.*) Shh! Answer the question, Karan Chand.
          What is your greatest wish?
          (*Pause.*)
          Is it for something in this room? No? Then is it for someone in this
          room? It is, isn't it? Who is it? It's not Amrita, it's not Deepak, it's not
          Chitra, it's certainly not me. Then who is it? Say it, Karan Chand!
          Say it!
MAMU:     I . . . I . . . Ansuya, don't go to Bombay . . . don't leave me!
RAI SAHEB:   Got you!
ANSUYA:   Mamu! What are you saying?
          (*Everybody starts speaking at once. They make exaggerated gestures to
          each other throughout the ensuing dialogue between Ansuya and Mamu,
          until Ansuya's outburst, when there is a sudden silence.*)
AMRITA:   What's this?
RAI SAHEB:   Dirty old man! This is incestuous. I always knew it.
DEEPAK:   (*Out of his depth.*) I say, yaar . . . What the hell's going on, yaar?
CHITRA:   Shameful! With his own niece!
AMRITA:   Are you mad, Karan?
MAMU:     Ansu, forgive me. You must not leave me, please!
ANSUYA:   Why are you doing this, Mamu?
MAMU:     Ansu...

ANSUYA:    (*Screaming.*) No, Mamu, no!

MAMU:    I . . . I . . . can't live without you.

ANSUYA:    Stop it, Mamu.

MAMU:    Ansuya!

ANSUYA:    (*Outburst.*) No! I'm Deepak's!

(*Sudden silence. Ansuya begins to cry.*)

CHITRA:    Deepak's?

ANSUYA:    You made me say it, Mamu. I love Deepak.

CHITRA:    *Yeh kya ho raha hai?*

DEEPAK:    I'll explain, Ma. Later.

ANSUYA:    I'm sorry, Deepak. I had to say it.

MAMU:    It's because he's young.

ANSUYA:    Mamu!

RAI SAHEB:    Filthy, I say. Abusing his own sister's trust.

MAMU:    (*Wailing.*) No, no! Oh God! Not that! I never . . .

AMRITA:    (*In a strange, high-pitched voice.*) I want everyone to be quiet. Please. This is my house, my brother and my daughter. I will speak. You fine people, what are you trying to do? We have lost everything. Why are you trying to destroy my family? It's all that I have left. We've lost the way we lived. But there was a time . . . oh yes, there was a time. But it is gone now. All we have left is ourselves, the three of us. Why must you judge us? We have suffered, and we drew close to each other in our suffering. You are trying to take even that away...

(*Pause.*)

Yes Chitra, the chandeliers, the paintings are gone. For you, they were things—things to be bought and sold for money. But for us, they were our life and the way we lived. We were happy once upon a time, and we didn't ask for any more.

(*Pause.*)

You Bunty, you have shattered everything. Yes, behind your laughter, respectability and pretence, I suddenly see you as you really are. And I do not like what I see! I thought you were a friend.

(*Pause.*)

I feel lost. I feel I am breaking bit by bit. But don't worry for me: I shall do what is right. I am tired now. No more games, please. I want everyone to leave. I wish to be alone with my family.

(*Exit Rai Saheb, Chitra and Deepak.*)

Why did you have to spoil it all, Karan? You have to leave now. You cannot live in this house any longer.

ANSUYA:    *(Going to her.)* Amma . . .

AMRITA:    Help me to my room, Ansu.

ANSUYA:    Come, Amma, come.

   *(Ansuya takes her mother inside. Fade.)*

# Act Four

[*Stage Centre. Opens on Karan, the narrator.*]

KARAN:   It's a dangerous game these girls play in boarding school. The
next time you have company, I wouldn't play this game, if I were
you. I know, games are a good way to get people off our hands—
especially people to whom we have nothing to say. Sometimes, even
ourselves. But, do you see the perils of playing games with people?
All of us take pride in being practical, realistic people. As realists we
have our feet planted solidly on the ground and we plod along,
fulfilling our duties, busy with our daily routine. And, at the end of
the day, what have we lost? We have lost the essence of life itself.

That is why Ansuya was such an unusual girl. She was willing to
take risks with herself: with her emotions, with her life. She wanted
something out of the ordinary, something different—and she wanted
love, in all its lurid splendour and terrible proportions.

And Deepak? Well, it's not as if he did not love Ansuya; he did, in his
own way. But his vision of himself was cradled by that apocalyptic
mother-figure, Chitra. I suppose we all want love, like Ansuya. We all
want romance to touch our lives at least once in our lifetime. Because,
love is, among other things, the best way to escape the primal loneliness
we were born to suffer. It is the one thing that makes our strange situation
in the world acceptable. Yet, we don't want too much of it, lest it
becomes a necessity, like alcohol. And, where there is love, there is pain,
a mighty pain. For love isn't love, unless it is vulnerable. And its loss is
a terrible thing. Those who say that death is worse, just don't know.

Mamu found that out as he left the house the next morning. He
wished he could die, and the almost intolerable torment was that he
did not.

   (*Picks up the newspaper.*)

Meanwhile, as the Chinese were digging in for a thrust at Se La and
Bomdilla, we are pointing fingers at each other. General Kaul and
General Thapar didn't see eye to eye on strategy. Krishna Menon
was not sure that we needed American aid. Do you know something?
Some of us talk too much and act too little.

It is the afternoon of the next day. A bright, fresh, sunny afternoon.
The house is still, taut with tension

(*Sniffs again, taking short breaths.*)

From the aroma in the kitchen it appears that it is almost tea-time.
It's so quiet that you can hear yourself breathing. Wait, someone is
talking in the drawing room.

(*As the lights come on.*)

It is Deepak and Ansuya.

(*Fade on Karan. Exit.*)

ANSUYA:    (*Withdrawn, distracted.*) . . . I took Amma to her room and then
I must have dozed off in the chair beside her. I was half asleep and
then I was dreaming . . . I can't be sure, but it was a bad dream. Mamu
kept calling me. I was at the bank and he was in the lake, or was it a
river? He kept calling me to save him.

(*She begins to cry.*)

He was drowning and I couldn't reach him. Oh, it was horrible. He
kept calling me.

DEEPAK:    (*Soothingly.*) It was only a dream.

ANSUYA:    You know dreams; things get mixed up. I took off my clothes
and I jumped into the water. It was cold. The wind was blowing.
The blanket kept slipping off.

DEEPAK:    Was there anyone else in your dream?

ANSUYA:    Yes.

DEEPAK:    Who?

ANSUYA:    I don't know. I don't remember, but I was scared.

DEEPAK:    There was no one there.

ANSUYA:    There was. I was naked and I didn't want anyone to see me.
The blanket kept slipping.

DEEPAK:    (*Changing the subject.*) How are the others?

ANSUYA:    Amma has been alone in her room all day. Mamu was up all
night and, early this morning, he quietly left for the station. I'm afraid
for him. My poor, dear Mamu.

DEEPAK:    What time did his train leave?

ANSUYA:    Ten o'clock.

(*Pause.*)

I am afraid. What will I do if something happens to him?

DEEPAK:    Don't worry. Nothing will happen to your Mamu.

ABSUYA:    You have such a lovely voice, Deepak. It is so sure and confident.
It gives me strength.

*(She goes up to embrace him. He withdraws slightly.)*

DEEPAK:    Ma should have been back from the club by now.

ANSUYA:    You and your mother . . .

DEEPAK:    It is late. She should have been back. How long do these lunches last, yaar?

ANSUYA:    What about us, Deepak? When are we going to tell everyone?

DEEPAK:    Tell what?

ANSUYA:    About my going to Bombay.

DEEPAK:    I have to speak to Ma.

ANSUYA:    But I have to ask Amma too.

DEEPAK:    Wait, let me speak to Ma first.

ANSUYA:    You sound scared.

DEEPAK:    No, yaar.

ANSUYA:    What's wrong? You were so sure last night. Deepak, tell me about Bombay and your ideas about the hotel. It will cheer us both up.

DEEPAK:    I'm tired, Anu.

ANSUYA:    What's the matter?

DEEPAK:    Nothing.

ANSUYA:    I want to hold you.

*(She goes close to him. Again, he withdraws.)*

DEEPAK:    I'm tired.

ANSUYA:    Let's go to Bombay.

DEEPAK:    What's the hurry, yaar?

ANSUYA:    Let's go away quickly.

DEEPAK:    Why?

ANSUYA:    I don't want to lose you.

*(Sounds of footsteps outside.)*

DEEPAK:    That must be Ma.

*(Deepak gets up at once, straightens himself. Ansuya gets up to leave. Chitra walks in with a brisk step. She is high, looks pleased with herself, and speaks louder than necessary)*

CHITRA:    Oh, there you are, Deepak. Oh, and Ansuya too. You know Deepak, I almost fell over that cat. *Bahut chalak hai.* It seemed to laugh at me. *Maine bhi use zor se thudda mara. Saali bhaag gayi.* (*Hiccup.*) A wonderful man, Rai Saheb! (*Hiccup.*)

DEEPAK:    You've been drinking again, Ma!

CHITRA:    *Kya mard hai,* Deepak! I tell you, you won't find another one like him. No wonder he is such a big government officer (*She pronounces* it 'gourmint ufsar.' Giggles and recalls her dance steps from the previous evening.)

One, two three; one, two three. Oh Deepak, *kya* life *hai, kya* manners! (Hiccup.)

DEEPAK:   And now you're drinking during the day?

CHITRA:   (Winking.) Oh-ho, *thodi si to pi hai!*

DEEPAK:   And what's happened to your clothes, Ma?

CHITRA:   (Smiling.) A bit crushed, are they?

DEEPAK:   They're a mess.

CHITRA:   (Her eyes light up.) Son, it is done. Your future is pucca, and your licence *meri mutthi mein hai!*.

DEEPAK:   You did not ... Oh Ma, you shouldn't have . . . I would have taken it up with Rai Saheb myself in course of time.

CHITRA:   *Kya hua maine kar diya? Ek hi to baat hai.* But Deepak, that is not all . . . I have some very big news for you! Oh, *main to khushi se paagal ho jaungi!*

DEEPAK:   What is it, Ma?

CHITRA:   Deepak, I have found a girl for you.

DEEPAK:   What?

CHITRA:   *Haan beta! Maine tere liye bahut hi vadhiya kudi dhoondh li hai!*

DEEPAK:   Ma, what are you saying? I . . . I've given my word to Ansuya.

CHITRA:   Kya? Ansuya? *Yeh kya bak raha hai?*

DEEPAK:   Ma, I've given my word to Ansuya.

CHITRA:   But last night you said . . .

(Looks at Ansuya and draws Deepak aside, away from her.)

Last night you said that you were only talking.

DEEPAK:   I had to say that to keep you from blowing up.

CHITRA:   *Achcha!* To keep me from blowing up? Well, I am going to blow up. I am going to blow up! How dare you commit to this . . .?

ANSUYA:   Deepak, I am afraid.

CHITRA:   You sneaky thing! *Jab se hum is ghar mein aaye hain, tu mere bete par dore dalne ki koshish kar rahi hai!*

DEEPAK:   Ma, please!

ANSUYA:   That's not true.

CHITRA:   I know her kind. Oh, madam, look at yourself. How old are you? *Haan?* How old are you?

ANSUYA:   Twenty-six.

CHITRA:   Well, let me tell you, you look thirty! Too old for my son!

DEEPAK:    Ma, what are you saying!

CHITRA:    *Tu beech mein mat bol!* Money hungry, that is what she is.

ANSUYA:    I don't want anything.

CHITRA:    Oh really? Don't want anything? Well we want, madam, we
           want! Look at you! No hips! No hips! How are you going to give us
           a son? Haan? No hips!

DEEPAK:    (*Screaming.*) Stop it Ma, stop it this instant!

ANSUYA:    (*Weeping.*) I can't take this anymore!
               (*Exit.*)

CHITRA:    Stop it Ma? All these years I've been teaching you: don't marry
           beauty; don't marry for love; marry a rich girl!

DEEPAK:    But I love her, Ma.

CHITRA:    He doesn't listen to me. 'Don't marry a beauty; don't marry
           for love . . .'

DEEPAK:    Yes, Ma, I heard you, '. . . marry money.' But, on the train up
           here, you said yourself that you wanted me to think of marrying
           Ansuya.

CHITRA:    That was before I found out that they had become poor.

DEEPAK:    Ma, I'm doing well. What do we need more money for?

CHITRA:    Oh-ho, we always need more money. There's never enough.
           Oh, *tu kya jaanta hai*, what it is like to grow up poor. What do you
           know what it was like to be tenants of these people in Lahore? *Kisi ke
           tukdon par palna, tu kya jaanta hai?* After Partition, what do you know
           what it was like to be a petty kiranawalla's wife in Ghatkopar?
               (*Disgust in her voice.*)
           Ghatkopar!

DEEPAK:    (*Cutting her short.*) I know. I know all that. Don't start it again.
               (*Pause.*)
           Ma, don't you care about what I want? Don't you care about my
           happiness?

CHITRA:    Oh beta, I care only about your happiness. I always have. *Jab tu
           itna sa tha, to din raat ek kar ke tujhe padhaya-likhaya. Khud bhookhi rah
           kar tera pet bhara. Tujhe is layak banaya jahan tu aaj khada hai* . . .

DEEPAK:    And this is happiness?

CHITRA:    (*Animatedly.*) *Achcha beta, yeh gussa chhod de.* Don't you want to
           know who I've found for you?

DEEPAK:    (*Wearily.*) No, Ma.

CHITRA:    *Yeh changa munda hai!* After all I have done for him . . .

DEEPAK:    (*Wearily.*) You'll tell me anyway.

CHITRA:    All right, I will tell you. Deepak, Rai Saheb has a niece. I think she is just the right match for you!

DEEPAK:    Who?

CHITRA:    Rai Saheb's niece! Look Deepak, you won't find another match like her. *Beta, beta, thande dimag se soch.* My guess is the dowry is not going to be under two lakhs. And maybe they will also give a car, a fridge and an air-conditioner. Uff! *Main to khushi se paagal ho rahi hoon!* I don't think I shall be able to sleep tonight, Deepak.

DEEPAK:    (*Bored and tired.*) What about the girl, Ma?

CHITRA:    *Hain?*

DEEPAK:    What about the girl?

CHITRA:    I didn't meet her.

DEEPAK:    She forgot the girl.

CHITRA:    Beta, I have seen her photo. Now look, they are in a rush. We shall have to act fast.

   (*Pause.*)

Well, aren't you going to say anything?

DEEPAK:    (*Matter-of-factly.*) I'm tired, Ma.

CHITRA:    (*Stunned.*) You are tired?

DEEPAK:    Yes, Ma, I'm tired.

CHITRA:    *Achcha!* Here I have been slaving for him—and the burra saheb is tired.

   (*Hurt.*)

I thought you would be jumping. Think of your future, son. When they find out about her in your company, you will probably get a double promotion.

DEEPAK:    (*Barking.*) To hell with my promotion, Ma. I want Ansuya.

CHITRA:    *Yeh phir shuru ho gaya!*

DEEPAK:    It's my one chance for an honest life. She is a fine person, with ideals, Ma.

CHITRA:    Oh-ho, that girl is only after your position and your job. She has trapped you, you simpleton. Deepak, think of your future. She doesn't have a naya paisa to her name. You're on the way up, son. Your star is going to rise. You need a rich girl to help you climb up. Her family are on the way down. She should be satisfied with a municipal clerk.

DEEPAK:    (*Resigned.*) You will never understand . . .

CHITRA:    I want my son to rise above the stink of his father's life.

DEEPAK:  No, Ma.

CHITRA:  (*Sarcastically.*) No, Ma? *Theek hai beta, theek hai. Aaj to tu bahut sayana ho gaya hai na? Apni Ma se bhi zyada! Theek hai.* You bring up a boy with all your love you snatch from the father to give to the son.

DEEPAK:  You were wrong to do that.

CHITRA:  (*Not comprehending.*) You bring him into the world in suffering. You feed him from your own breast. You stay awake at nights so that he can sleep. And when he wets the bed, you pick him up and put him on the dry side and yourself sleep on that wet side.

You wear the same dirty rags, so that he can go to school.

DEEPAK:  Enough, Ma!

CHITRA:  No! Do you know what I have done for you today?

DEEPAK:  What?

CHITRA:  *Main abhi kahan se aa rahi hoon, tujhe pata hai?.*

DEEPAK:  Yes, yes, I know. You went to the Club with Rai Saheb.

CHITRA:  *Haan. Rai Saheb ke saath gai zaroor thi.* But not the Club. To his house. *Ek ghanta unke saath bita kar aa rahi hoon! Samjhe?*

DEEPAK:  What? You mean . . .? (*The realization of what she has done dawns on him.*)

No, Ma! No!

CHITRA:  Oh, yes!

DEEPAK:  (*Horrified.*) No, Ma!

CHITRA:  Oh, yes, Ma!

DEEPAK:  God!

CHITRA:  What a mother will not do for her own son! And this is my reward, ji. After all my sacrifice, I get a pauper for a daughter-in-law. It is a fate worse than death. *Tu ja, ja—us hoor pari ke saath gulchharre uda.* Just do one thing before you go—take me to the ghat and perform my funeral!

(*And she begins to howl. Slowly the howling gets louder.*)

DEEPAK:  Quiet Ma, please!

CHITRA:  (*Sitting down and wailing*) *Main to lut hi gayi! Lut hi gayi!*

DEEPAK:  Shh…please!

CHITRA:  *Aa, beta, aa!* Let me tell you something. We'll get only one pandit, and save money! In the morning he will marry you, in the evening he will burn me. *Beta*, there's a knife lying there. Bring the knife, and cut my throat with it.

DEEPAK:  (*Suddenly losing control.*) Quiet, Ma!

*(Deepak collapses on the floor near his mother. Clearly, something has snapped within him.)*

You'll have your way! You always have!

*(Lights begin to change gradually as Deepak changes into a little boy.)*

Ever since I was a little boy. I was a regular teachers' pet, the kind everybody hates. I would come running home from school, clutching 80 per cent marks in my hand, the good little boy, endlessly in search of the key to that deep and inscrutable mystery, the approval of his mother. Oh, yes, I was Ma's good little boy.

*(He mimicks his mother.)*

'Who is the best little boy any Ma ever had? Who does Ma love more than anyone in the world?' Me!

*(Turns away from Chitra. The lighting has become a cold, white spot, as Deepak becomes a little boy.)*

I'm seven. Ma cooks for me, Ma cleans for me, Ma stays up late at night for me, Ma cares for me when I am sick. Ma waits for me after school and when I come home, she asks, 'Who is the best little boy any Ma ever had? Who does Ma love more than anyone in the world?' 'Me, me.'

*(Sobbing. Chitra gets up, goes behind Deepak, takes his head in her lap. Slowly, he comes out of his trance.)*

Look, Ma. I'm giving up Ansuya! I'm giving her up and my one chance for happiness. I'm doing it for you. And I feel sick to my stomach.

CHITRA:    *Mera beta.*

DEEPAK:    I've lost, Ma! I've lost.

CHITRA:    *Mera raja beta.*

DEEPAK:    Am I a coward, Ma?

CHITRA:    *Yeh tu kya kah raha hai?*

DEEPAK:    You taught me to go after success, Ma. And I did. You forgot to warn me there might be others in the way. I'm your puppet, Ma. Pull the string. Pull it harder. Choke me.

CHITRA:    *Mera achha beta. Mera raja beta.*

*(Fade. Next evening. The same scene. Ansuya is helping Amrita pack. There are boxes and wrapping paper and string all over the floor.)*

ANSUYA:    Pass me some paper, Amma.

AMRITA:    Here! Do you think we should take this Bengal pottery vase with us?

ANSUYA:    No, Amma dear. We should take only the nice things.

AMRITA:    Yes. You're right. So many things accumulate in a house over the years.

(*Pause.*)

Ansu, it is wonderful to see you up and about like this.

ANSUYA:    When is the truck coming?

AMRITA:    Saturday morning, Ansu. With the way things are, I cannot bear to live in this house any longer.

ANSUYA:    Did I say anything in my sleep, Amma?

AMRITA:    Everyone was so worried. Poor Dr Nath, such a darling man! He stayed by your bed all night.

ANSUYA:    How embarrassing, Amma.

AMRITA:    I spent the night with you. With Karan gone, it was suddenly so lonely. I've never felt so alone in my life, my child.

ANSUYA:    Amma, we need some more string.

AMRITA:    It's there, right behind you.

(*Pause.*)

I must learn to laugh and cry at the same time. It's the only way I can hide the fact that I know the difference between the way things are and the way they might have been.

(*She gets up, goes to the window, and looks out.*)

Ah, my sweet Ansu. I am going to miss Simla. I used to be intoxicated, just breathing its air. There was something about every day—whether it was sunny or raining.

ANSUYA:    You can still have Simla, Amma.

AMRITA:    It will not be the same, will it, my darling?

ANSUYA:    No, it won't.

(*Pause.*)

AMRITA:    Ever since this morning, the brokers started to hound me about the house. I was so confused. I didn't know who to turn to.

ANSUYA:    Pass me some more paper, Amma.

(*Amrita picks up the paper and gives it to her. She hugs her daughter.*)

AMRITA:    Oh Ansuya, I'm so glad you are well.

ANSUYA:    But, when I woke up, there was no Deepak in the house.

(*Smiles sadly.*)

The fool, he could at least have said goodbye.

(*Pause.*)

AMRITA:    They dined at Rai Saheb's last night and left this morning.

ANSUYA:    (*Pause.*) Did he get engaged last night?

AMRITA:    Ansu . . .

ANSUYA:    Did he, Amma?

AMRITA:    You must forget him, child.

ANSUYA:    Did he get engaged?

AMRITA:    Yes.

ANSUYA:    So, the Rais finally did manage to find poor Neena a husband.
           (*She turns to hide her tears.*)

AMRITA:    My sweet Ansuya. There, there . . .

ANSUYA:    The truth is, Amma, I think this is what Deepak really wanted.
           Don't blame his mother. For Deepak, it was always his career above
           everything.
           (*She goes towards her daughter. But Ansuya withdraws. She slowly gets
           up and goes towards the window. Long pause. Slowly and resolutely, she
           turns around to face her mother. The tears are gone. She comes forward
           with a deliberate step, with a raised head, to centre stage.*)

ANSUYA:    Don't worry about me, Amma. Yes, I broke down last night.
           But it will never, ever happen again.
           (*Pause.*)
           I've been thinking, Amma. All day, I've been thinking. I'm going to
           be strong. I'm going to look after you. This house will never be sold!
           That's why I threw out the brokers this afternoon.

AMRITA:    (*Smiling.*) Ah, that explains why they suddenly went away.

ANSUYA:    You might as well put up a 'Not for Sale' sign outside. I am
           going to follow up on Deepak's idea. I'm going to Bombay. I am
           going to talk to the people at the Taj. And, I'm going alone.

AMRITA:    But . . .

ANSUYA:    No 'buts,' Amma. Now, you must leave it to me. We are not
           going to stand helplessly by and become poor. I am now taking
           charge. I shall prove to you that I can do it. I shall not rest until you
           are secure. I want you never to worry about money, ever again.

AMRITA:    Oh, my child, you give me so much strength.

ANSUYA:    I've learned a lot in these three days, Amma. I used to believe
           that people like us couldn't do anything. But I'll show them. Yes,
           Deepak showed me the way. I shall make it happen.
           (*Suddenly, she has tears in her eyes.*)

AMRITA:    What is it, my darling?

ANSUYA:    Amma?

AMRITA:    Yes, my child?

ANSUYA: I ache for Deepak.

AMRITA: I understand, Ansu.

ANSUYA: Amma?

AMRITA: Yes?

ANSUYA: I'm in pain.

AMRITA: My child.

ANSUYA: It hurts too much.

AMRITA: I know.

ANSUYA: Amma?

AMRITA: Hm?

ANSUYA: Will the pain go away?

AMRITA: In time, my child.

ANSUYA: I love him so much.

(*Pause.*)

In the midst of our desperate, killing boredom, Deepak came like a rainbow.

AMRITA: It is going to be quiet with just the two of us.

ANSUYA: Yes.

(*Pause.*)

No, Amma. You mustn't say that. It's not going to be quiet. We have work to do. We are not going to cry. We are going to build. I shall show you the way.

AMRITA: (*Wearily.*) Yes, we mustn't look back. I suppose we'll have to live in Delhi now.

ANSUYA: Now pass me those books, Amma.

AMRITA: Perhaps it won't be so bad, after all.

ANSUYA: We need a bigger box for the books, Amma.

AMRITA: Yes . . ., yes . . ..

(*Fade.*)

# Epilogue

[*Stage Centre. Karan, the narrator.*]

KARAN: So there it is: a story, among so many, of the Partition of the country, but more, of partitions in the mind. What more can I say?

The Chinese withdrew from India after three weeks, for reasons no one understood. Seventeen months later, Nehru died. I was in Nagpur when it happened. With him died many of our dreams. Not only ours, but those of half of India's as well. And an era came to an end.

Things were never ever the same for our splintered family. People like us—Amrita, Ansuya and I—we became creatures of the past. The Deepaks and Chitras of the world took charge of the future. Deepak became the Managing Director of his company and he gave glittering parties, over which Chitra, and not his wife, presided as the hostess.

I became a writer after I was . . . after I left the house. This play was written last year. As you can see, it's autobiographical. And I wouldn't be honest if I didn't admit that writing it helped me to get her out of my system.

Oh yes, our house did become a successful hotel, thanks to Ansuya. She worked tirelessly, like someone possessed, to make Deepak's idea come true. It solved Amrita's money problems, finally. But none of us ever went back there again. 9 Jakhoo Hill, our home, was lost forever.

Thank you, once again, for having come to see the play. Good night.